just 10

just 10

THE TEN COMMANDMENTS
STUDY GUIDE

J.John

Authentic

MILTON KEYNES ● COLORADO SPRINGS ● HYDERABAD

First published 2009 by Authentic Media
9 Holdom Avenue, Bletchley, Milton Keynes, MK1 1QR, UK
1820 Jet Stream Drive, Colorado Springs, CO 80921, USA
Medchal Road, Jeedimetla Village, Secunderabad 500 055, A.P., India
www.authenticmedia.co.uk

Authentic Media is a division of IBS-STL UK, limited by guarantee, with its
Registered Office at Kingstown Broadway, Carlisle, Cumbria CA3 0HA.
Registered in England & Wales No. 1216232. Registered charity 270162

British Library Cataloguing in Publication Data
A catalogue record for this book is available from the British Library

ISBN: 978-1-86024-761-3

Scripture quotations are taken from the Holy Bible, New Living Translation,
copyright © 1996, 2004. Used by permission of Tyndale House Publishers, Inc., Wheaton,
Illinois 60189. All rights reserved.

Cover Design by Chris Jones
Print Management by Adare
Printed in Great Britain by J F Print Ltd., Sparkford, Somerset

CONTENTS

INTRODUCTION

Over the last few years I have been preaching on the Ten Commandments. Nothing could have prepared me for the extraordinary interest that has greeted these talks. In the moral wasteland of the Western world in the twenty-first century there is a clear hunger for instruction on what is – and isn't – right.

Some of this interest has come from those from outside the church. As the muddy torrents of secular and New Age values have surged through society, link after link between Christianity and popular culture has been washed away. One of the few bridges remaining above the floodwaters is that of the Ten Commandments. Although most people would struggle to name more than two or three of them, they know that the Ten Commandments still exist. They know too that they gave previous generations a moral certainty that our own age so spectacularly lacks.

Yet there has also been enormous interest from within the church where even Bible-honouring churches seem to have fought shy of the hard task of ethical teaching. One comment from the group on whom these studies were tested was revealing. When they came to discuss the matter of honouring parents, as covered by the Fifth Commandment, it emerged that – despite a combined total of over a hundred years of regular adult churchgoing – no one could remember a single sermon on the topic.

Now the reasons for the neglect of the Ten Commandments are complicated. One of them is that actually applying these ancient commandments is far from easy. There are two gaps that have to be bridged. One gap is that of culture; our complex technological world is very different from that of Moses and the Israelites. We are not nomads living in extended families in a semi-desert environment. The other gap is the religious gulf; these commandments were given to God's covenant people who he had delivered from Egypt and to whom he had promised a land of their own. Keeping the Ten Commandments was for the Jews the appropriate response to God's act of freeing them out of slavery. Christians, however, live in the light of the Cross, not the Exodus. We are New Covenant people and these commandments have a different relevance to us than they did to the Old Testament Jew.

The best way of bridging both gaps is, I believe, for us to sit down and work through prayerfully and thoughtfully what the word of God says to us and what it means for our lives. Now you and I could do this on our own in the privacy of our own homes. While this would be good, the experience of many generations of Christians is that actually the best way of studying the Bible is as part of a small group. Small group Bible study is especially good for encouraging the virtues of perseverance, clarity and honesty that can be in short supply when we study the Bible on our own.

- The presence of the questions and the interaction with other people forces us to persevere in understanding hard passages. On our own it is all too easy to give up on difficult (or demanding) passages and to move on.

- The act of answering questions and expressing those answers publicly encourages clarity. We are forced to come to terms with what the passage actually says. Equally, the viewpoints of other people can make us see a Bible passage afresh.

- Above all, perhaps, small group Bible study forces us to be honest with ourselves. If we glance at, say, 'Do not murder' it is all too easy for most of us to shrug our shoulders, say 'no problem' and dismiss the commandment. In the small group context we are forced to grapple with what this really means.

Once you have studied these timeless values, there's space in this book to make a written record of your personal journey as you discover the practical power of God's blueprint for life.

THE BASIS OF THESE STUDIES

There are different types of small group Bible study. Some use tightly focused questions with a single right answer to trace a well-marked path from which no deviation is allowed. Their advantages are those of microwave meals; they are easily prepared and they are relatively foolproof. Their disadvantages are, however, also those of microwave meals; they tend to be bland and unmemorable and they often don't suit the needs of your particular group. In reality a 'one-size-fits all' Bible study never really fits anybody.

These studies are different. Many of the questions are designed to elicit thought and reflection rather than the 'yes or no' answer. In fact – and here I reveal a secret – I believe that the best sort of Bible study is not simply about getting right answers to questions. It is actually about training people to get those answers themselves. It is helping people to get into good habits of reading the Bible and applying it to their lives. A Bible study is not about feeding sheep, it is training sheep to feed themselves and, ultimately, to train other sheep.

As a result there is a considerable degree of flexibility built into these studies. In fact I have put tick boxes by many of the units so that leaders can mark which of them they actually plan to use. The existence of this flexibility does mean that the leader (on whom more below) has to work harder to spend time on the material, picking, choosing and – if needs be – modifying the questions. In a separate section at the end of each study I have put supplementary material. The extent to which you use this material depends on how long your group spends on each study. Some people may also find it helpful as 'homework' or as a source for private study material.

HOW LONG SHOULD WE SPEND?

The idea is simple and obvious; there were Ten Commandments so there would be ten studies. Easy! Yet, even as these studies were being written, doubts emerged. For a start the issues that each commandment raised were complex. There was the need to balance the Old Testament teaching with the New Testament material from both the gospels and the letters. Above all the material required participants to think hard about what these commandments meant for them in their workplaces and their homes.

When these studies were tested these doubts were justified. The topics proved to generate such interest and discussion that even by discarding a lot of material it proved to be impossible to cover the ground adequately in an hour or even an hour and a quarter. Again and again the demand came back; we need more time to discuss this. The solution was to break the material into two so that each commandment was covered over two weeks. Doing a commandment over a fortnight also had the incidental benefit of allowing people a week in which to reflect on what was being discussed. So the study section of each commandment is divided into two parts. Part One is essentially the introduction and the Old Testament material while Part Two is the New Testament material and the application. The only potential problem is that if people miss a week then they could – in theory – get a distorted view of a commandment. Hopefully leaders will be aware of this and will try to fill in the gaps. Besides, if all participants have study guides then they can catch up.

Now you could, if you really wanted, do the entire study in ten weeks. By sticking to the 'Group Study' questions, cutting back on the starter and avoiding diversions you might be able to do it. But in even suggesting doing a commandment a week I feel as if I'm recommending how to do the sights of London in just one day. It's just scratching the surface and it is likely to leave you exhausted rather than enthusiastic. If, despite my cautions, you do decide to do the commandment-a-week option what I would suggest is that participants use the tick boxes to mark the material covered and try to do the remainder later in their own time.

STUDY ELEMENTS

Each study is divided into the following components. The suggested timings are based around a 75- to 80-minute long study time.

Starter: This is a short warm-up activity, mainly for the first week of each two-week study. Only gently challenging, it is designed to put everybody at ease and to get them talking. On the recommended two-weeks-a-commandment schedule, spend no more than 10 minutes on this. Any material not discussed there could be used in a brief warm-up the following week.

Surgery: This section highlights with facts, questions or statistics some of the problems that this commandment addresses. In terms of timing I would allow no more than 10 minutes on week one.

Study: This is the heart of the material and is the one that occupies most of the time. With each commandment there is a division into two parts: an Old Testament and a New Testament section. For this I suggest you allow a maximum of 60 minutes.

Summary: This is a short review section which tries to bring together some of the conclusions that have emerged during the study. For this you really ought to allow at least 10 minutes in the second week.

Stepping out: This is the 'So what?' section. It is a series of suggestions, thoughts and questions to try and encourage participants to apply the commandments in their own lives. You should allow at least 10 minutes in week two.

In terms of timing don't worry about having too much time. First of all, it's very unlikely and, secondly, there is supplementary study material provided that you can bring in. The wise Bible study leader will have prepared an extra question or two from this just in case.

PRACTICALITIES

To do these studies you need three things: you need a venue, a copy of this study guide for each participant and you need a leader.

The venue should be somewhere where people can feel comfortable, after all the demands the Ten Commandments make are uncomfortable enough. The ideal situation is a cosy room in a friendly house with an ample supply of soft chairs and refreshments. If phones can be diverted and shouting toddlers occupied elsewhere, so much the better.

It is also a good idea to have enough copies of this study guide. If people do not have a copy of their own then the leader will often have to repeat the questions and, as time is at a premium, this is a distraction. There are at least two advantages to everybody having their own book. First, it allows for preparation before the study and if people are prepared then that will greatly help. Second, it allows for the follow-up after the study. The way these studies are structured means that – even on the preferred two-week programme – it is quite likely that there will be material that the study has not been able to cover. If participants tick off what has been done they can do their extra material at their leisure.

The leader is critical. Someone needs to be designated to be in charge; without leadership you are all too likely to get sidetracked. You could decide on a leader for the whole course or you could have an alternating leadership. Do bear in mind that, if you go for the twenty-week option, it is a near certainty that everyone will miss at least one or two sessions. In other words, you will need a backup leader. The role of the leader is vital and I have included some guidelines below. Here it is worth saying that it is best if the leader and the host (or hostess) can be two different people. It is almost impossible to make the refreshments, open the door, take phone calls and lead the study.

PARTICIPATING IN BIBLE STUDIES: SOME ADVICE

Much of what I want to say here is probably obvious to you but I think it bears repeating. I think the advice can be filed under the three great biblical words faith, truth and love.

Have faith. There is a time and a place for hard questions about the nature of the Bible text (Can I believe this? Are our translations correct? etc.) but a Bible study is not it. The traditional Christian belief is that when we have a Bible in our hands what we hold is God's written word to us, inspired and preserved by the power of the Holy Spirit. We will get most profit in Bible study if we believe that this is indeed God's word and that in it God speaks to us. In a Bible study it is not us that judges the text, it is the text that judges us. This position of faith in the text is not naive credulity ('just believe'); it is a position that can (and has been) carefully and logically argued. It also has its own internal logic, after all no interaction with a person is going to be successful unless there is some degree of trust in his or her truthfulness.

Have honesty. These Bible study groups deal with real life issues and they can get painfully close to the bone. Be careful that you do not slip into the classic defence of human beings when faced with a moral challenge, deciding that it only applies to other people. So be watchful that, say, a discussion about theft does not come to centre on how a particular class of people (perhaps politicians or builders) are thieves. Unless we are politicians, builders or whatever, that sort of thing only makes us feel smug. Be honest with yourself. Let the light shine in the dark places of your life.

Have love. This is most important.

- Think of the others in your group all the time. Let them speak, encourage them and, where you can, build on their comments.

- Be sensitive to the wounds others may have. For instance, it is easy for men in particular to sound off about the sin of abortion. But there may be women in the group who have had one and are coming to terms with the guilt. Think before you speak, lest your words hurt and wound.

- Don't come down heavily on others, even when you know they are wrong.

- Treat what has emerged in these meetings in total confidence.

- Between study meetings, pray for those that meet with you around God's word.

SOME SPECIAL ADVICE FOR BIBLE STUDY LEADERS

All the above comments especially apply to leaders. But there are some special things that I want to say to you. First of all, as a general point, remember you don't have to be a spiritual or intellectual giant to lead a small group Bible study. Actually it helps to be normal; the best leaders are those who can stay in the background and who supply the questions and keep a study on-track and on schedule. It is even better to be humble too and a servant of all.

Now let me give you some bits of advice.

Pray! It is good to begin and end the study with prayer. How exactly you do this is up to you and it may take time for the right pattern to emerge within your group. A typical format would be for either you or someone else to open with a short prayer specifically asking God's blessing and help on the study. Then at the end you could have a longer, more open time of prayer. This might involve points raised by the study as well as items for prayer and praise. It is also good to encourage prayer in the intervening week for the study group.

Do your homework. Other people may be able to come to study cold; a leader shouldn't. You at least ought to make sure that you have read the passage and checked over the questions and read the notes I have put in for the leaders (see Text Conventions p.14). There are decisions you need to make; for example which of the alternative passages are you going to study? Which of the optional starter questions are you going to use? There are lots of good background articles and books that you can read to help you. You may find my book *Ten, Living the Ten Commandments in the 21st Century* (Kingsway, 2000) helpful. Incidentally, if you have prepared to the extent of having read the commentaries (good) and studied the Greek and Hebrew originals (awesome), try not to flaunt it. This is a Bible study, not *Mastermind*.

Stimulate but don't dominate. The ideal Bible study is where everybody contributes. Your task as leader is to facilitate this; you are not a lecturer or guru. This may involve gently directing questions to those who are hesitant to speak or encouraging them to elaborate their hesitant answers. It may also involve gently discouraging those who subconsciously (or consciously!) want to dominate the group. Your own aim should be to be unobtrusive. The really great Bible study leader is one who leads so well – and in such a low-key way – that the participants don't even notice that they are being led. Needless to say being the invisible man or woman is not a task that we naturally like.

Work hard. Leading a Bible study properly allows for little relaxation. You need to constantly listen to what people are saying. Someone may make a comment that needs development; that may be the cue for you to ask them to expand it. Sometimes it is the non-verbal language that is important; the twisting of the fingers that suggests that someone really wants to say something, or the stiff back and distant stare that reveals that someone is feeling threatened by the discussion.

Be sensitive. This is particularly important with these studies on the commandments. Here, as we study the word of God, we must expect that God's Spirit may convict us in a way that we find uncomfortable. Sometimes it may become evident that some people are finding the questions or comments painful. What do you do? I think the issue is whether it is God or a human being that is doing the hurting. The temptation is always to soft-pedal on some of the more demanding Bible passages, yet the last thing you want to do is dilute what God is saying to someone. But for some people it may be that it is the study rather than the Spirit that is doing the hurting. In this case you may feel it right to move on and to try and have a private conversation later. In the back of your mind you may want to ask yourself 'What counselling resources can I draw on if this subject raises deep issues in someone's life?' There are also practical matters to watch. For example, never get the group to read round a passage unless you are sure that no one has a problem with reading aloud. People with a literacy problem such as dyslexia can easily be embarrassed this way.

Be patient. Sometimes it can seem to take forever before anyone answers a question. Resist the temptation to answer it yourself unless it is absolutely necessary. If no one wants to answer the question then try and rephrase it or break it down into components.

Stay focused. The general rule is this: know where you want to go and when you want to get there and then go for it. Don't get sidetracked. Now to do this you may have to put your foot down in places. One person may want to have a learned theological discussion; someone else may want to bring in a rambling anecdote of little relevance. Try and bring things back on course and here tact and humour often help. There is, however, an important exception to this rule of being goal focused. That is where something emerges that is clearly so important that you feel it would be irresponsible to terminate the discussion. Almost certainly this will not be a purely intellectual question – where the dinosaurs fit into Genesis 1 can definitely wait – but it will be one that is a heartfelt burden. Here a brief diversion may be justified.

Aim for a good spirit. Positively, that means trying to get people to interact with each other in a friendly and loving way. Negatively, it means damping down any awkward or inappropriate interactions. For example, try not to let the discussion get hijacked by arguments over Bible versions, church structures or other secondary issues.

SOME OTHER COMMENTS

A) THE ORDER OF THE STUDIES

You will notice immediately that these Bible studies start with the Tenth Commandment and move down the list to the First Commandment. This is a deliberate and thought-through choice rather than an act of mental perversity. It is in fact the order I have followed in my series of talks on the Ten Commandments and that I have used in both *Ten, Living the Ten Commandments in the 21st Century* and the *10+ Service Outlines* book that is the companion to this volume. The reason for this arrangement is as follows. The Ten Commandments were originally given to the Israelites as part of the covenant agreement with God. He had created them, led their ancestors and just recently dramatically rescued them from slavery in Egypt; he now promised to love, guide and protect them for ever.

The Ten Commandments were the outline of the responses God expected from his people to that love. Let me give you an analogy. Imagine an orphan is rescued out of misery and poverty and adopted by a family. As the child settles into the new home, slowly getting used to the love and acceptance that now surrounds them, the family rules will be gradually spelt out to them. This, the child's new parents will say lovingly, is how we do things here. The original hearers of the commandments would have understood that what was being given them were the obligations that were now expected of them as God's rescued and adopted covenant people. They were – if you like – on the inside of the covenant looking outwards.

Now modern men and women do not come to the commandments from anything like the same position. Most of us come to the commandments – if we come at all – as strangers to the idea of a God who loves, rescues, adopts and makes covenants. We are on the outside of the covenant looking in. For such people to start with the First Commandment with its demand for unconditional and total worship of the one God, the LORD, is too much. It is far easier in my experience for modern men and women to start in the shallows of the Tenth Commandment before being eased gently into the deep waters of the First Commandment with its demand for exclusive worship.

Of course you may disagree and you can change round the order easily enough. But at least now you have my reasons.

B) WHICH BIBLE VERSION?

Although these questions were written around the text of the New Living Translation, which has been used for the quoted passages, the questions all fit with the New International Version too. Either version is satisfactory, and probably most modern translations (such as NRSV and GNB) will work well. Although I have a great deal of respect for the King James (or Authorised) Version I find that in group Bible study it tends to be distracting because so much effort goes into simply trying to understand the language.

C) ALTERING THE STUDY CONTEXT

These studies were written during 2000 for a UK audience, a fact inevitably reflected in some of the illustrations and statistics and in some of the questions. In fact, it seems that study material can either be sharply focused or be of universal scope; but to make it both is almost impossible. If you are using these studies for another culture it should be relatively easy to update questions to make them more appropriate and relevant for your own setting. You may also want to insert extra questions to address specific issues in your own culture. Mind you if you do, try not to use them to grind personal axes!

D) TEXT CONVENTIONS

The following basic and largely self-explanatory conventions are used in the text.

❑ Tick box for marking material you plan to do or have done.

Note: Italicised text like this is a general comment.

> NOTE: Boxed text like this is a comment mainly for leaders.

STUDY 1
FIND TRUE CONTENTMENT

Commandment 10: *'You must not covet your neighbor's house. You must not covet your neighbor's wife, male or female servant, ox or donkey, or anything else that belongs to your neighbor.'* (Exodus 20:17)

Some people would like to drop some of the Ten Commandments because they are too hard or because their demands on us are too severe. The tenth commandment, however, is one that people feel could be dropped because it doesn't seem worthwhile. 'Do not covet!' It doesn't seem fair to put it in the same category with commands dealing with murder or adultery. After all, who was ever hurt by our coveting? Besides, wouldn't our modern economy collapse without us coveting things? In fact very few writers on ethics, apart from those who treat the Bible seriously, even bother mentioning coveting. Yet, as we shall see, the importance of coveting is much greater than we might think at first.

PART ONE

1) STARTER

First, get everyone involved in the following two exercises:

a) How much money would it take to get you all you want? Decide on a definite figure and share it with the person next to you. Make sure they remember the amount. ❑

b) Imagine a modern British family of four, made up of two working adults with two teenage children. Each member of the group should take, or be allocated, one of the following areas of their lives. After time to think (maybe over coffee) each person should speak very briefly (definitely for no more than a minute) on the things that they might feel were desirable or ideal to have in the area allocated to them. While there are no real financial constraints don't go completely over the top!

The areas are:

Housing
Holidays
Transport (cars/bikes etc)
Music systems/MP3 players
TV/DVD set-ups including games consoles
Computing facilities

Kitchen equipment
Other household equipment
Storage and bathroom facilities
Insurance/pension, etc. ❏

Now

a) Imagine that a new government has decided to make the Ten Commandments legally enforceable. The group leader has been made Minister Responsible for the Tenth Commandment and needs some advice. Suggest:

- How he or she can enforce this commandment?

- What penalties should they introduce for coveting? ❏

b) If you go shopping in a big city what is it that brings your expedition to an end? Is it shortage of time, money, energy or enthusiasm? Or is it when you can't carry any more? ❏

Now review the figure that you said earlier would get you all you want. Is it is still enough? What happened?

2) SURGERY

Discuss at least one of the following:

a) If aliens observed a medieval British city they would probably have concluded from the size and architectural magnificence of the cathedral and the numbers of people that visited it that Christianity was the major force in the lives of the inhabitants. If they were to look at a modern British city on the same basis what would they probably conclude was the focus of our beliefs? ❏

b) The slogan of the age is 'I want more'. But isn't that just putting a positive spin on the despairing statement 'I can't get enough'? ❏

3) GROUP STUDY

This is divided into an Old and a New Testament part.

The Old Testament

a) This commandment is about what we desire in our hearts. The following three passages talk about different desires. Listen while three people read out Psalm 37:4, Song of Solomon 7:10 and 1 Kings 8:57–58.

- What sorts of desires are talked about here?

- Are they wrong? ❏

b) Read Exodus 20:17.

- From the examples given, exactly how would you explain what this sort of desire is?

- If this commandment was being written today what equivalent examples would you give?

- Why do you think the examples are of things like these, rather than, say, coveting your neighbour's looks, youth and happiness?

- Today the concept of marriage is dominated by the idea of sex and romantic love and the notion of coveting your neighbour's wife (or in our day, spouse) in the same way as their ox or house seems grotesque or even offensive*. Yet sexual desire is covered in the Seventh Commandment so this is presumably directed at something else.

  - Have we ever wished to possess someone else's wife or husband as a possession or an acquisition?

  - When a married person has the sort of thought that goes 'Oh, I wish my husband had his intelligence' or 'I wish my wife would dress like she does' is this breaking this commandment? Is this a real temptation? (Warning marrieds: think twice before answering yes!) What are the inevitable effects of such thoughts on a marriage?

  (It is more common than we imagine for people to see a spouse at least partly in terms of an acquisition. How often have you heard someone say something like 'a trophy wife' or 'she made a good catch' or 'he married well'?)   ❏

NOTE: The Hebrew word here 'to covet' really means 'desiring to possess'.

---

* Note: Some people may feel concerned that this commandment supports the inferior status of women. The following, however, should be noted. A) Whilst women in Old Testament culture did have fewer rights than men they were never treated as property; for example wives could never be sold. In fact the Fifth Commandment 'Honour your father and mother' implies a degree of equality. B) There is a difference between addressing a particular cultural situation and endorsing it. God's ideal for marriage can best be seen in Genesis 2:18–24 where the woman is the man's companion and, above all in the New Testament where marriage is used as imagery for the loving and sacrificial relationship between Christ and the church.

4) PERSONAL STUDY

a) Read Genesis 3:1–6.

- How does the serpent (the Devil, see Revelation 20:2) encourage Eve to covet?

- According to v.6 what three elements go into Eve's coveting of the forbidden fruit?

- Is coveting the first sin? If so what does that tell us about its significance?   ❑

b) Read 1 Kings 21:1–19.

- Why does Naboth refuse the king?

- As King, Ahab presumably was not short of land, so why doesn't he accept Naboth's refusal with good grace? What does the fact that kings covet tell us about the power of coveting?

- What effect does this refusal have on the king? What has coveting given rise to? Have you ever known similar symptoms?

- Jezebel takes matters into her own hands. What others of the Ten Commandments now end up being broken?

(As Elijah prophesies, the ultimate results of this affair are disastrous for Ahab and Jezebel and both they and their dynasty come to spectacularly bloody ends. After the study you might want to read what happened in 1 Kings 29:35–38 and 2 Kings 9:21–37.)   ❑

NOTE: In the Old Testament, land was meant to stay with the family (Leviticus 25:24–28, Numbers 36:7).

SUMMARY OF PART ONE

If, as recommended, you are spreading the study of this commandment over two weeks, try to end the first week here by summarising what you have learnt from the Old Testament passages you have studied. What issues have they raised?   ❑

PART TWO

REVISION OF PART ONE

If, as recommended, you are spreading the study of this commandment over two weeks, it is useful to try and spend a few minutes here reviewing what you learned the previous week in Part One before moving on to the New Testament.

5) GROUP STUDY

The New Testament

Jesus spoke more strongly than any one before (or after) on the sins of the heart, and coveting and greed did not escape his attention.

   a) In Mark 7 we read how Jesus was criticised because his disciples did not perform the Jewish rituals of ceremonial handwashing. Jesus replied strongly and then turned to address the whole issue of cleanliness. Read Mark 7:14–23.

- Where, according to Jesus, does sin not come from?
- Where, according to Jesus, does the root of sin lie?
- How significant then is our thought life? ❏

   b) Read Luke 12:13–21 where Jesus is asked to intervene in an inheritance dispute.

- How in verses 14 and 15 does he specifically reply to the request?
- What does Jesus say real life does not consist of? What do you think he would say that it does consist of?
- What does the rich man in the parable promise himself that his wealth will give him?
- What does he overlook? What danger does this suggest is attached to covetousness? ❏

6) PERSONAL STUDY

   a) Read Matthew 6:19–34.

- Why, according to Jesus in verses 19–24, is concentrating on earthly treasures both foolish and dangerous?
- Why are we not to covet even those things that are our needs?
- If we covet, who are we like (v.32)?
- What is our real priority to be? ❏

b) Read Matthew 19:16–22. In his response Jesus lists most of the commandments but omits the Tenth Commandment.

- How does the man respond initially? Are you impressed? (I am).

- Why do you think Jesus doesn't ask him about whether he keeps the tenth commandment but gives him (in v.21) a direct order?

- What does this suggest about the influence and extent of coveting in our lives? ❏

c) Read Mark 12:28–31.

- If we covet can we seriously say that we are keeping the first of the great commandments?

- If we covet our neighbour's possessions can we seriously say that we are keeping the second of the great commandments?

- If we covet things are we likely to feel generously inclined to our neighbour? ❏

The rest of the New Testament develops Jesus' teaching.

7) GROUP STUDY

a) Read Romans 7:7–9. Paul's main argument here is that the Old Testament Law made him aware of sin, a fact that was specifically brought home to him by the Tenth Commandment.

- The Jewish religion that Paul had held firmly to before his conversion concentrated on keeping God's Law by behaving in the right way. Why might this commandment have revealed the inadequacy of this system? ❏

b) Read Colossians 3:5.

- Paul links covetousness (or greed) with what other class of sins? Why?

- Paul says greed is idolatry. In what ways is desiring things like the worship of a god? ❏

8) PERSONAL STUDY

a) Read James 4:1–3.

- What are the symptoms of the problem James describes?

- What does James think is the underlying disease?

- What is the solution? Is it that God will give us whatever we want?

- On the basis of this passage what are the sorts of requests to God that he will reject? What are the requests that he will honour? ❏

b) Read 1 Timothy 6:6–10.

- According to Paul does the real danger of coveting lie in it being a sin or in it being the doorway to sin?

- What is his alternative to coveting? ❏

c) Read Philippians 4:11–13 and remind yourself that Paul was in chains (see Philippians 1:13) as he wrote this.

- What might Paul have coveted?

- How was he able not to covet?

- What seems to have been his secret of contentment? ❏

9) THE SUMMARY

a) Think about coveting:

Coveting affects things. How does coveting affect our relationship

- With God?

- With people who are wealthy?

- With people who are poor? ❏

b) Think about contentment:

Define contentment.

- Is it to be found in a) having many things, b) having enough things c) or does it have nothing to do with things at all?

- How does coveting relate to contentment?

- How can we find contentment? ❏

c) Discussion

We need to think how this commandment is applied. Try and talk through at least two of the examples below.

i) Do we ever fall into the trap of thinking that physical things will make us happy and that they can provide us with satisfaction, peace and joy? ❏

ii) You have seen something that you really badly want but you realise that you don't really need it. It has preoccupied your thoughts. Suddenly you find you have a tax rebate of exactly the amount to buy it.

Do you:

- go ahead and buy it?
- give the money away to avoid the temptation?
- invest the money?
- give away at least a tenth of it? ❏

iii) Are we asking for trouble to go shopping when we don't actually need anything? Aren't we asking to be tempted? ❏

iv) We are surrounded by advertisements that seek to try and make us want things we don't need. What should our response to these be? ❏

v) Imagine that someone in your church has just bought a very expensive car.

- Can we assume that he or she has broken this commandment?

- Can we ever determine whether someone has slipped into this sin?

- But are we to say nothing in church about the sin of coveting? ❏

d) So what?

At the end of this study:

- What has challenged you most?

- In what areas are you most prone to breaking this command?

- What do you need to change?

- What do you really want to work on? ❏

10) STEPPING OUT

a) Practical suggestions

- Practise the habit of recognising thoughts of coveting.

- Try to ignore advertisements. Skim over them in the paper, don't linger on them. When you are watching TV and a commercial break occurs, turn the sound down.

- Distinguish between your wants and needs. Then examine your needs to see whether they are things that are seriously needed.
- Practise contentment; praise God for what you have rather than be concerned about what you do not have.

b) Further study

Do any of the studies that you have not done so far.

i)   Read Matthew 16:24–26.

- According to these words can we follow Jesus and covet?
- What does Jesus offer us in this life instead of worldly wealth?
- What does Jesus offer us in the next life instead?
- Is life, according to Jesus' definition, more about giving up rather than gaining?   ❏

ii) Read James 1:12–16.

- Can we blame God for our covetous desires?
- What is the end result of coveting?   ❏

c) Questions to think about

i)   For private contemplation only. What fills our minds in our spare moments is often what we really worship. If a 'mental video' of your mind could be shown over the last twenty-four hours, what might it suggest to be your god?   ❏

ii) For private contemplation only. Which do we look forward to most? A time of worship or fellowship or a good day's shopping?   ❏

iii) Should you feel guilty if you work in advertising or in making products or clothes that are designed to be attractive?   ❏

iv) The Buddhist answer to coveting would be to get rid of desire altogether. Is this a) the right answer? b) even possible?   ❏

v)   How do we share the good news of Jesus with someone whose life revolves around 'possessions'?   ❏

STUDY 2
HOLD TO THE TRUTH

Commandment 9: *'You must not testify falsely against your neighbor.'* (Exodus 20:16)

If the Tenth Commandment was about invisible and weightless thoughts, this commandment is about things that are only slightly more substantial: words. Yet although words can reveal truth and bring comfort, more often than not they hurt, enrage, tempt and above all, deceive.

PART ONE

1) STARTER

First, do one or both of the following:

a) Try to find as many words in spoken and written English as you can for 'not telling the truth'. (For starters, how about fiction, telling fibs, telling a story . . .) What does this suggest about how widespread lying is? ❏

b) Allocate everybody one of the following scenarios. Give them a chance to think about them (perhaps over refreshments) then get them to talk for a full minute.

- You are a defendant in a law court. Explain why you had possession of a scanner, a high quality colour printer and a book entitled *How to Literally Make Money*. ❏

- You are manager of the local soccer team. Explain why you were beaten 6–0 by the team at the bottom of the league. ❏

- You are the PR officer for a car-manufacturing firm. Represent, in the best possible light, your firm's decision to recall your latest model because it has an engine fault that allowed it to catch fire. ❏

- You are head of a political party. Put the best possible spin on your disastrous performance in a recent by-election. ❏

- Explain to your spouse why you failed to get five out of the ten shopping items that you were sent for. ❏

- A police officer wants to know why you drove into a wall. The reality is that you were concentrating on trying to get the wrapper off a very sticky toffee. ❏

- You are a holiday tour operator. Explain how an unfinished construction with no hot water a full twenty minutes' walk from the sea came to be labelled as a deluxe beachside hotel with full facilities. ❏

Second:

Try to answer together the following:

- Why do we lie?
- How easy did you find it to lie, mislead or distort the truth? ❏

LEADER'S NOTE: The point of this warm-up is to point out 1) that lies are common, 2) most lies are told to shift guilt from us and 3) it is amazingly easy for us to slip into telling lies.

---

2) SURGERY

Discuss at least one of the following:

a) You are applying for a job and are filling in the career history section of the application form. This is tricky because for twelve months you took a job where you performed so badly that you were fired. Consider the following possibilities:

- Mention the job, but have an excuse ready if they ask you at interview.
- Fail to mention it and hope they will overlook the time gap.
- Alter the dates of employment of the jobs either side so it never existed.
- Invent a totally fictitious job to fill in the gap.

Which is lying? Which is merely 'not telling the truth'? Which of the possible responses do you think is the most wrong? Why? ❏

b) In what areas of private and public life today have people found 'truth-decay' a problem? Give examples of statements or situations where in people's experience they have found that:

- Not all the facts were told.
- The facts were told but in a way that misrepresented reality.
- A total and complete fabrication was presented. ❏

LEADER'S NOTE: Be careful! After all you may have a used car dealer or a politician in your study group.

---

c) Imagine you work with X and one day he or she calls in sick. Later on that day you have to go into town and you see them shopping. How does that affect your subsequent relationship with them?   ❑

3) GROUP STUDY

This is divided into an Old and a New Testament part.

The Old Testament

a) Read Exodus 20:16.

- To testify also means to be a witness. In what sorts of settings today do we use words like testify and witness? What sort of common abuse do you think this commandment is primarily addressing? In a society where many of the legal judgements involved the death penalty, why would a false accusation be so serious?

- Are there limits as to whom we define as our neighbour? (See Luke 10:29–37.)

- Is this only about making false accusations in court? Or might it also include a failure not to speak in defence of someone when we could do so?

- Is the Bible here concerned about the philosophical nature of what truth is? Or is it concerned about the practical cost of lying?   ❑

b) Read Genesis 3:1–13.

- Consider what the serpent (the Devil, see Revelation 20:2) says in verses 1 and 4. How does he misrepresent: a) God, b) God's rules, c) the results of disobeying God?

- Look at the responses of Adam and Eve in verses 12 and 13? Are they totally truthful? What are they trying to avoid?   ❑

> NOTE: Try to avoid the questions of where and when this took place. You may also like to mention that Jesus calls the Devil 'a liar and the father of lies' (John 8:44).

c) Look up the following verses in Isaiah:

- Isaiah 65:16, Isaiah 45:18–19. What do they tell us about God's character in regard to truth?

- Isaiah 59:12–15. What do these tell us about human character in regard to truth? ❏

d) One Hebrew word used in the Old Testament to do with truth is one we all know: Amen. This is a solemn response that basically means 'truly!'

Read Nehemiah 5:13. Here the prophet has just commanded the people to stop being unjust.

- When the people make a response of 'Amen' to these words is this just an admission that what Nehemiah has said is intellectually true?
- Christians frequently say Amen at the end of prayers or hymns or sermons. But if we had to translate this word into modern English what words might we use instead? When we do say Amen do we really mean anything? Shouldn't we treat the word more seriously? ❏

NOTE: This may seem slightly peripheral to the idea of truth and false witness. In fact it is setting the scene for Jesus' remarkable use of Amen.

SUMMARY OF PART ONE

If, as recommended, you are spreading the study of this commandment over two weeks, try to end the first week here by summarising what you have learnt from the Old Testament passages you have studied. What issues have they raised?

PART TWO

REVISION OF PART ONE

If, as recommended, you are spreading the study of this commandment over two weeks, it is useful to try and spend a few minutes here reviewing what you learned the previous week in Part One before moving on to the New Testament.

4) GROUP STUDY

The New Testament

Jesus said very strong things about the truth.

a) In the Old Testament we find over four hundred places where the prophets began their message with the solemn formula that is translated as 'The LORD says' or 'thus saith the LORD'. However, Jesus never used this phrase in his teaching; instead he often used the word Amen at the start of his sayings. In older versions this was translated into English as verily but in most modern translations it is translated as 'for I tell you the truth' or 'I assure you'. There are around a hundred occurrences of this in the gospels and it appears to be something that was unique to Jesus.

- Read as examples (perhaps shared out among the group) Matthew 5:18, Mark 12:43, Luke 18:17, John 1:51 and John 8:58.

- Why, when there was a perfectly good formula for prophets to use, do you think Jesus chose to use this way of emphasising his words?

- What does this say about his commitment to the truth?

- What reaction did this produce among his hearers (Matthew 7:28,29)?

- What reaction should it produce in us?   ❏

LEADER'S NOTE: In John's gospel Jesus uses a double version and says Amen, Amen. This is probably not a significant difference but some study members may notice.

b) Truth is a major theme in John's gospel.
    Read John 14:6.

- What does Jesus say about his relationship to the truth?
Read John 8:31–32.

- How do we find the truth? Why do we need to find the truth?
Read John 18:37–19:3.

- What do we learn in v.37 about Jesus' commitment to the truth?

- What do we learn in v.38 about Pilate's commitment to the truth? ❑

NOTE: Some people have read Pilate's query about truth sympathetically, as if he was a frustrated philosopher. However, his feeble attempt at trying to get Jesus a reprieve followed by his ordering of an extremely brutal punishment suggests it was more of a dismissive sneer than a serious enquiry.

---

c) There is much more teaching in the New Testament about telling the truth.

- The 'last word' on liars is to be found in Revelation 21:8 and 22:15. What does this suggest about the seriousness of failing to tell the truth?

Read John 16:13.
- With Jesus gone how can his followers know the truth?

Read Ephesians 4:14–25.
- How are we to hold to truth (v.15)? What should that make us like?
- What is the relationship of Jesus to truth (v.21)?
- How should knowing him affect our lives with regard to truth (v.25)? ❑

5) THE SUMMARY

a) Think about lies:

- How have we seen that the Bible views the telling of lies?
- One form of lying that is strongly attacked in the New Testament is hypocrisy, where we pretend to be – or even think that we are – good. Why is this sort of self-deception disastrous? Why is it better to be a sinner aware of your sin than one who is ignorant of it?

- What is the effect of lying in the following areas:
  - Our relationship with God?
  - Our relationship with other people?
  - Our ability to assess our personal state?
- Do we treat lying as lethal? ❏

b) Think about truth:
- How does the Bible value truth?
- How can we know the truth?
- How can we best follow the truth?
- How can we become more transparently honest? ❏

c) Discussion

We need to think how this commandment is applied. Try and look at a couple of examples from all three sections below.

i) Think about the following situations:

- You have seen a new clothes fashion on the TV that you think is just ridiculous. You arrive at a friend's house and they rush to the front door wearing exactly that item. What's more, your friend looks ludicrous in it. They ask you what you think of it and whether they look good in it. What do you say?

- You have been looking forward for ages to a quiet night in. However, when the time eventually comes the phone rings just as you sit down to relax. As you go to answer it your spouse says, 'If it's for me, tell them I'm not in.' It is; what do you say to the caller?

- You see a serious traffic accident. Do you volunteer to be a witness knowing that you may be involved in a long and tiresome court case or do you pretend you saw nothing? Is your failure to speak a false witness?

- You go shopping for a particular item and find that out of ten items one has a very much lower price marked on it. When you take it to the till do you point out the difference in pricing? ❏

ii) Discuss whether the following actions break this commandment:

- Pretending to forget someone's birthday in order to surprise them.

- Responding 'Oh fine!' when asked, 'How are you?' when you are feeling lousy.

- Letting children believe in Santa Claus.

- Telling an angry drunk who is banging on your door that his wife is not around when, in fact, she is hiding in your kitchen.

- Making a film or writing a novel that – without warning the audience – plays fast and loose with historical facts. ❏

iii) Does this commandment have anything to say about:

- Gossiping?

- Making hurtful or insulting comments to people?

- Keeping secrets? ❏

d) So what?

At the end of this study:

- What has challenged you most?

- In what areas are you most prone to breaking this command?

- What do you need to change?

- What do you really want to work on? ❏

6) STEPPING OUT

a) Practical suggestions

- Should you as an individual become accountable to someone? Is there anyone you can think of that you could give permission to ask the hardest questions and you wouldn't lie? What would you need to know in order to be able to have this kind of accountable relationship?

- Could you as a group commit yourselves to having a rule that you did not say something unless it had passed the THINK test?
  T   is it True?
  H   is it Helpful?
  I   is it Inspiring?
  N   is it Necessary?
  K   is it Kind? ❏

---

b) Further study

James 3:1–12 is the classic passage on the control of the tongue.

- What bit of this strikes you most?
- What bit of this is the hardest to keep?
- Do you think it is really that hard to tame the tongue?
- Can you remember a time when you have been hurt by another person's words?
- Do we treat words too lightly? ❏

c) Questions to think about

i) If we doubt something that God has plainly promised us (like forgiveness of our sins in Jesus) aren't we accusing him of lying? ❏

ii) All Christians are called to be witnesses to the good news of Jesus. Are we by our words and actions faithful witnesses? If not, are we breaking this commandment? ❏

STUDY 3
PROSPER WITH A CLEAR CONSCIENCE

Commandment 8: *'You must not steal.'* (Exodus 20:15)

Theft is enormously widespread, occurring for many reasons and in many ways. Theft is linked with the two commandments we have discussed earlier. Theft occurs where coveting goes from thought to action and, if it does not involve actually lying, it almost always involves a readiness to lie. We are all affected by theft; we all condemn it in others, yet it is something that we all too easily find that we have committed ourselves.

PART ONE

1) STARTER

First,

a) Go round the group asking people to come up with the first image that comes to mind when the word thief is mentioned. ❏

b) Each of the following paragraphs describes a pair of people who may (or may not) have committed theft. Each member of the group should be allocated one pair to read aloud. The others then have to decide whether or not they are guilty of theft.

- Andy is self-employed, on a low wage and failed to declare a fifty-pound contract to the Inland Revenue. Annabelle is in charge of the corporate finances of a company and managed to hide nearly a million pounds of earnings from the Inland Revenue last year.

- Bill is a car salesman who, in order to raise the price of an old car, has had a careful paint job done to hide serious rusty patches. Beryl is desperate to sell her house and has failed to mention a badly leaking roof.

- Charlene has made an unauthorised personal copy of a software package produced by a small family firm whose profits are only a few thousand pounds a year. Clive has made a copy of an overpriced software package produced by a multinational firm whose profits are nearly a half a billion pounds a year.

- Doug owns a firm in an area where there is high unemployment and hires people at the national minimum wage. Denise buys in components from a factory in the developing world for her business, knowing that the labourers there must be being paid no more than a pound a day.

- Ellen created a pension scheme that wiped out the investments of many elderly people. Ed ran a financial scam that deprived a drug dealer of his life savings.

- Acting on the leaked news of a business takeover, Fred made fifty thousand on the stock market overnight. Frances, after twenty years of careful investing in stocks, has just made fifty thousand pounds.

- Gwen has her house robbed but by exaggerating her losses makes a profit out of the insurance claim. George is a builder who dumps his rubbish in the countryside rather than paying the council to dispose of it.

- Harry works in the corner shop and helps himself to chocolate bars when he feels like it. Heather owns a new supermarket that takes the corner shop's custom and puts it out of business.

Not easy, is it? ❑

Now

a) How many different types of stealing can you come up with? How would you define theft? ❑

NOTE: A typical dictionary definition of 'to steal' would be 'to take away illegally or dishonestly something belonging to another, especially secretly and with no intention of returning it'.

---

b) What is the opposite of theft? ❑

NOTE: The intention of this starter is to discover 1) that theft is extraordinarily widespread and hard to limit, 2) that there are grey areas where it is hard for us to judge and 3) that it is extremely subtle.

---

2) SURGERY

Discuss at least one of the following:

a) Theft is a major problem. In England and Wales in the twelve months up to March 2006 there were 644,049 recorded offences of burglary and 1,975,389 cases of theft of (or from) vehicles. How many of the people in the group have been the victims of car or property theft? ❑

b) We have become used to a high level of theft in our society. If all theft ended today what changes would we be able to make in how we live? How much time, effort, money and worry would we save? ❏

c) Who has been strongly tempted to steal something but resisted? Why were you tempted? Was it a hard temptation to fight? ❏

3) GROUP STUDY

This is divided into an Old and a New Testament part.

The Old Testament

a) Read Psalm 24:1 and Leviticus 25:23.

- Who owns everything?
- What status does that give us?
- Do we actually own anything?
- How does that affect our attitude to what we call our possessions? ❏

b) Read Exodus 20:15.

- Why, in a rural culture existing close to poverty level, is theft so serious?
- What are the effects of theft within a community? Why would it be vital that theft did not occur within the Israelite community? ❏

c) 'Theft' covers many things. Have different people read out the following verses. After each one is read out ask yourselves: i) What type of theft is being condemned? ii) What would an equivalent modern example be?

- Exodus 22:25–27
- Leviticus 19:13
- Deuteronomy 19:14
- Isaiah 10:1–2.
- Amos 5:11
- Amos 8:4–6

What is it about theft that seems to displease God so much? ❏

4) PERSONAL STUDY

a) Read Exodus 22:1–6. The detailed laws given here represent examples of how the principle of this commandment was to be worked out in practice.

- In verses 1–4 what guidelines (exacting revenge, deterring future offenders or making restitution, etc.) seem to be used to determine the appropriate penalty for theft?

- Elsewhere in the Near East at this time (and, in places, today) theft had a penalty of death or mutilation attached (e.g. lopping off a pickpocket's hands). The Old Testament took a different view on property crime. What does this suggest about how God views the relative value of property and people?

- Verses 5–6 cover property loss caused by carelessness; what we might call 'theft by accident'. What did these rules try and achieve? ❏

b) The Old Testament laws were not just simply 'against theft' but also aimed to create a society in which the necessity to steal in order to survive was eliminated. Read Deuteronomy 15:1–11.

- What attitudes were the Israelites to have towards the poor (verses 8,9,10)?

- What was to happen to loans at the end of seven years (v.1)?

- From Leviticus 25 we find that even if someone had to sell their ancestral land, it had to be returned in the Year of Jubilee (at the end of the 49th year). What effect on Israelite society would these rules on the 7th and 49th years have had? ❏

NOTE: Exactly how the loan system worked in ancient Israel is not known. The key point seems to be that this law was a limiting mechanism to stop the poverty spiral where the poor got poorer and poorer.

---

c) The Old Testament also celebrates and praises personal generosity. Read Job 31:16–21. Here Job, afflicted by suffering, protests his innocence.

- Why is there the emphasis here (already seen) on widows and orphans?

- If Job were living today what would he say? ❏

---

d) Read Proverbs 30:7–9.

- What does the writer ask God for?
- What is his concern about wealth?
- What is his concern about poverty? Why does it insult or dishonour God's name?
- Is this a prayer that we should pray?   ❏

e) Read Malachi 3:6–12.

- How had the people of Israel cheated God?
- Who were the losers?
- How can we cheat God?   ❏

SUMMARY OF PART ONE

If, as recommended, you are spreading the study of this commandment over two weeks, try to end the first week here by summarising what you have learnt from the Old Testament passages you have studied. What issues have they raised?

PART TWO

REVISION OF PART ONE

If, as recommended, you are spreading the study of this commandment over two weeks, it is useful to try and spend a few minutes here reviewing what you learned the previous week in Part One before moving on to the New Testament.

5) GROUP STUDY

The New Testament

In the New Testament all theft is treated as being wrong.

a) Read 1 Corinthians 6:9–11.

- Who are thieves linked with here?
- What is the bad news of this passage for thieves (v.10)?
- What is the good news of this passage for thieves (v.11)? ❏

b) Theft in some shape or form is a particular attraction when we feel that things aren't fair. Read 1 Corinthians 6:1–8.

- What was apparently happening in the Corinthian church?
- What attitudes seem to have been common?
- According to verse 7, what alternative attitude would Paul prefer?
- On this basis how should we respond to an injustice against us? ❏

6) PERSONAL STUDY

a) A common question is 'What should someone do who was financially dishonest but who has now become a Christian?' In Luke 19:1–10 we see an example of this. Here Zacchaeus has come into a right relationship with Christ.

- How do Zacchaeus's changed priorities show in his attitude to his wealth?
- How do his changed priorities show in his attitude to any former stealing? *Note: Zacchaeus would have taken a commission on any taxes he collected.*
- While there is no reason to treat the percentages involved here as binding (after all the rich man in Luke 18:18–30 was asked to give away everything!) what principles can we learn

about our attitudes to wealth and to our dealing with past wrongdoings? ❏

b) Read Ephesians 4:28.

- What is the converted thief to stop doing?
- What is he or she to do instead?
- How, according to this verse, is the general outlook of the Christian to be different from that of the non-Christian? ❏

The New Testament teaching on stealing goes further than simply condemning the wrong way of acquiring wealth. Jesus, in particular, talks much about the misuse of wealth. It also repeatedly encourages generosity.

c) Read Luke 14:12–14.

- Why does Jesus consider that being kind to those in our own social circle doesn't count as generosity?
- Who are we to be kind to instead?
- How could this work out in practice today? ❏

d) Read John 12:1–7.

- What was Mary's attitude to wealth?
- What was Judas's attitude to wealth?
- How can we imitate Mary? ❏

e) Read Acts 4:32–37.

- How did the early church seek to live out Jesus' teachings on poverty?
- What prompted them to sell land or property (verses 34–35)? ❏

NOTE: This does not appear to have involved the giving up of all private property (see Acts 5:4) but rather a willing sharing of all possessions and resources as needed.

f) Read 2 Corinthians 8:1–11.

- What characterised the giving of the Macedonian churches?
- Does Paul order the Corinthians to give in a similar manner? Why not?
- How does Jesus set an example for our giving?
- If giving is the focus of our lives, is theft likely to be an issue?

7) THE SUMMARY

a) Think about stealing:

- Why do we want to steal?

- If we steal, what does that say about our relationship with God?

- We may be careful about not stealing money or property from our employers but do we steal our labour from them? Do we arrive late, leave early, read novels on the job, make excessive personal phone calls, daydream or just cut corners on what we are paid to do?

- Are we honest in all our financial transactions? Bearing in mind the variety of ways that there are to steal, how can we be sure that we are innocent?

- If we have stolen, what should we do about it? ❏

b) Think about generosity:

- What does it mean to be truly generous?

- How is being generous something that ought to be natural and appropriate for someone who is a child of God?

- How would a policy of rich generosity affect our church life? ❏

c) Discussion

We need to think how this commandment is applied. Try and look at a couple of examples below.

i) It would be possible to use this commandment to defend the right of the rich to keep their property and wealth. But is that the right use of this commandment?

ii) In 1840 the French social reformer Pierre-Joseph Proudhon wrote that 'property is theft'. Is this the view of the Bible? If private property isn't theft, then what is it?

iii) Theft is a crime against the community and the Bible treats the concept of community more seriously than most of us do. Can theft and a real community coexist? Would you feel able to easily share your possessions and your life with someone who was a thief? ❏

d) So what?

At the end of this study:

- What has challenged you most?
- In what areas are you most prone to breaking this command?
- What do you need to change?
- What do you really want to work on? ❏

8) STEPPING OUT

a) Practical suggestions

- Can you look at everything that you have (including your bank balance) and say 'This is not mine, it has been given to me by God'? ❏

- If we believed we were accountable to God for things in our possession would we seek to have more of them or less of them? ❏

- How can you be more generous? ❏

b) Further study

i) Remind yourselves of the first sin (Genesis 2:15–17 and 3:1–6). We have already seen in Studies 1 and 2 how coveting and lying was involved with this.

- In what ways was theft also involved?
- Given God's generous nature (Adam and Eve could eat anything else in the garden) why was this a serious crime? ❏

ii) Read Leviticus 25:24–28.

- What would this piece of legislation prevent? ❏

iii) In the Old Testament, one form of theft is viewed as a capital offence. Read Deuteronomy 24:7.

- Given that Israel was a nation brought out from captivity in Egypt by God why do you think this crime is treated with particular severity? ❏

iv) Read Joshua 7:1–26. God had commanded the Israelites that, as they took over the Promised Land, the pagan towns should be set apart to him by their destruction.

- Why was Achan's theft so serious?
- We often think of sins like theft being a matter that purely affects the individual concerned. Is this the case here?
- If God had ignored Achan's sin what do you think would have been the moral effects on the Israelites?

A New Testament parallel to this is to be found in Acts 5:1–10 with the story of Ananias and Sapphira.   ❏

v) Read Jeremiah 7:8–15.

Jeremiah is prophesying at a time when the nation of Judah is under threat from foreign armies.

- According to verse 9 what sins are the people committing?
- How do they make matters worse (v.10)?
- What attitude do they have towards the temple?
- How does God view their trust in the security of the temple and their worship there?
- By this time Shiloh had been destroyed for centuries. What is God's warning to the nation through Jeremiah? *Note: In 587BC Jerusalem fell to the Babylonians and the temple was destroyed.*

Read Mark 11:15–17.

- Why, six hundred years later, did Jesus repeat Jeremiah's words?   ❏

vi) Read Matthew 25:31–46.

This passage talks about the great and final division of the righteous and the wicked.

- How have the righteous used their wealth?
- How have the wicked used their wealth?   ❏

vii) Read Romans 13:8–10.

- If we steal from someone what attitude do we have to them?
- If we love our neighbour as ourselves can we rob them?   ❏

viii) Read Philippians 2:3–11.

- What rights did Jesus have?
- What was his attitude to those rights?
- Why did he give them up?

- If we had such an attitude, how would it affect the likelihood of us being involved in theft? ❏

ix) Read James 5:1–4.

- Is James here opposing wealthy people in general? What is he condemning?
- What will happen to their wealth in this life? What use will it serve in the next life? ❏

c) Questions to think about

i) It is claimed that Robin Hood 'stole from the rich to give to the poor'. Is this a justifiable defence for theft? ❏

ii) What would the prophets denounce in our society today? ❏

iii) Could we implement some of the Old Testament ideas of not lending at interest and not owning property forever, today? ❏

iv) Present-day British law treats property crime as something that can – and often is – punished by a jail sentence. The Old Testament law demanded restitution of theft, if necessary by unpaid labour (slavery). Which is preferable? ❏

v) Isn't our destruction of the environment simply theft from future generations? ❏

STUDY 4
'AFFAIR-PROOF' YOUR RELATIONSHIPS

Commandment 7: *'You must not commit adultery.'* (Exodus 20:14)

PART ONE

1) STARTER

First,

a)   Either:

Ask who follows the TV soaps? In which of them is there a marriage on the rocks at the moment? What are the reasons for that failing marriage?   ❏

Or:

Below are two role-play sketches. You need two volunteers for each to play the two roles.

i)   Andy and Craig are having a drink. Andy has just left his wife Trish after ten years of marriage for a much younger girl, Clare. Craig has just heard about it and is curious; he has some sympathies for Trish. Andy is anxious to defend his actions.

CRAIG: 'So Andy, is it true what I hear about you and Trish?'

ANDY: 'Fraid so . . .'

Now continue the conversation for a few minutes.

ii)   Hazel and Di are talking over coffee. Hazel has had enough of Dave, her husband, and has finally walked out on him. Di is both appalled at the collapse of the marriage and curious to know why things have come this far.

DI: 'So you just had enough of him?'

HAZEL: 'I had enough . . .'   ❏

b)   Think of an unhappy marriage that you have known but were distant enough from to be fairly objective. When talking of them make sure that they are unidentifiable.

- Why was the marriage so unhappy?
- Were the problems only on one side?

- Why did they split up (or stay together)?
- Did the split help matters? ❏

c) Think of a happy marriage that you have known. (Although anonymity is less critical here it is probably the best policy).

- Why was the marriage so happy?
- Was it happy because there were no problems?
- Why did they stay together?
- How did they handle conflict? ❏

2) SURGERY

Discuss at least one of the following:

a) Consider the following figures (Source: One Plus One):

- 4 in 10 marriages in England and Wales will end in divorce if the current rate is maintained.
- Cohabitations are even more likely to break down.
- The public cost of divorce is over £4 billion a year; the cost to the typical British organisation through absenteeism and lost productivity is estimated at over £5000 a year for each divorcing individual.

Shouldn't these figures shock us? Why don't they? ❏

b) What effects of marriage break-up today have you personally witnessed in the lives of others? *Note: no names!* ❏

3) GROUP STUDY

This is divided into an Old and a New Testament part.

The Old Testament

Before looking at adultery and sexual sin it is important to understand how the Bible views marriage.

a) Read Genesis 2:18–25. Although Christians debate over how much of this language is symbolic, all are agreed that this passage sets out the foundations for all human marriage.

- What is Adam's need (vv.18,20)?
- How does the woman (later named Eve) fulfil that need? Does this passage suggest that the woman has a higher or lower status than the man?

- Verse 24 is effectively the Bible's definition of marriage and is quoted by both Jesus and Paul.
    - According to it, who are the two parties of a marriage?
    - What are the three actions that make up a marriage?
- According to this passage the sexual act results in the man and the woman being united or becoming 'one flesh'.
    - What does this mean?
    - How does it stand in contrast to the modern view that sex is no different from any other physical contact?
- What does verse 24 imply about:
    - Homosexual relationships?
    - A polygamous relationship where there is more than one wife or husband?
    - A sexless marriage?
    - A marriage where, for whatever reason, there are no children?
    - Sex without marriage?
- What do you understand by the statement in verse 25 that Adam and Eve were naked and had no shame?

Now look at Genesis 3, which describes how Adam and Eve rebelled against God and the results of that act of disobedience.

Read Genesis 3:7.

- What is the first indication to Adam and Eve that something is now wrong? What does this suggest about our sexuality?

Read Genesis 3:16.

- What has happened to the state of loving companionship between man and woman described in chapter 2? ❏

NOTE: Someone is bound to mention the fact that many of the men of the Old Testament were polygamous. While not banned, polygamy is never approved and it is never praised in the way that the monogamous marriage is. The accounts in the Bible of polygamous households often mention their tendency to be a source of tension (i.e. 1 Samuel 1:1–8) or temptation (i.e. 1 Kings 11:3).

b) The Song of Songs is a series of poems celebrating married love. Read Song of Songs chapters 6 and 7. Try not to be deterred by the lavish eastern imagery.

- Which of the senses are evoked in these words?
- Although some of the details are unclear what is this celebrating?
- 'They don't make poems like that any more!' True, but has our present society's preoccupation with the mechanics of sex damaged our ability to have romance?
- What does the fact that a poem such as this is in the Bible say about how God views sex? ❏

c) God uses marriage as an illustration of his solemn and unchanging covenant love for his people. In Ezekiel there are a series of graphic images of how God relates with his people, here termed 'Jerusalem'. Read Ezekiel 16:1–14.

- What was Jerusalem's position when God found her?
- What did God do for her?
- How does God describe the relationship between himself and his people?
- What does that tell us about God? What does that tell us about marriage?

Now read verses 15–17.

- What might God have expected from Jerusalem?
- What did Jerusalem do instead?
- What does God say is equivalent to prostitution?
- Why is this a powerful image? ❏

As we have just seen, the Old Testament's high views on marriage are matched by strong words about the sin of breaking marriage vows.

4) PERSONAL STUDY

a) Read Malachi 2:13–16.

- Why is God not accepting his people's offerings?
- What particular sin is God angry about?
- What do we learn about marriage from this passage?
- What do we learn about God's attitude to marriage? ❏

The Old Testament gives several examples of people who either failed or triumphed over sexual temptation. David and Joseph are the two classic examples.

b) At the start of 2 Samuel 11 David is king in Jerusalem and already has a considerable number of wives and concubines.* Read verses 1–26.

- List the steps through which David descends into adultery in verses 2–4. Where is the start of the sin? Was there a chance for him to stop the process?

- How do things become awkward for David? Why doesn't he just admit that he has sinned? What does he do instead?

- How is the character of Uriah contrasted with that of David?

- As part of his cover-up what other sins does David end up committing?

- What lessons can we learn from this about the danger of lust? ❑

Note: In 2 Samuel 12 you can read how Nathan the prophet visited David, brought him face to face with his sin and announced God's judgement on him. The catastrophic family problems that dogged David from this time onwards are seen in the Bible as being the results of the sins recorded in chapter 11. David's own confession is in Psalm 51: see Further Study.

c) Much earlier in history, Joseph was sold into slavery and taken to Egypt. Read Genesis 39:1–19.

- Joseph is a long way from home; why might a sexual adventure be an attractive option?

- How does Potiphar's wife successively attempt to seduce Joseph (verses 7,10,11)? How in each case does he resist?

- What reason does Joseph give for resisting (v.8,9)?

- What price does Joseph pay for his integrity?

- What lessons are there for us in Joseph's example? ❑

Don't worry, it all ends happily for Joseph! But the Bible gives no guarantees that this will always be the case.

SUMMARY OF PART ONE

If, as recommended, you are spreading the study of this commandment over two weeks, try to end the first week here by summarising what you have learnt from the Old Testament passages you have studied. What issues have they raised?

* Secondary wives with reduced legal rights

PART TWO

REVISION OF PART ONE

If, as recommended, you are spreading the study of this commandment over two weeks, it is useful to try and spend a few minutes here reviewing what you learned the previous week in Part One before moving on to the New Testament.

5) GROUP STUDY

The New Testament

The teaching of Jesus revolutionised the basis of marriage and sexual morality. This was partly through his direct teaching on the matter but also in the way that Jesus raised the status of women.

a) Read Matthew 5:27–32.

- What does Jesus do with this commandment? Why do you think he points the finger at the thought life rather than at the action?

- Does Jesus confine adultery to a physical act that breaks a marriage contract? On this basis can anyone be innocent?

- In recommending a solution, Jesus uses exaggeration for impact (after all, even the blind can lust), but what do his words suggest about the seriousness of lust? How does this contrast with our society's attitude?

- How can we adopt similarly radical solutions today? ❏

b) By the time of Jesus, divorce had, at least for the man, become easy. Read Mark 10:1–11.

- What, according to Jesus, was God's original purpose for marriage?

- Why does he say that a married couple ought not to be separated?

- What attitude to sex and marriage is Jesus seeking from his followers? ❏

c) Read John 8:1–11.

- Doesn't it take two to commit adultery? According to Leviticus 20:10 and Deuteronomy 22:22 the man should have been stoned as well.

  – What do you feel about his absence?

  – How do you think the woman is feeling?

- If Jesus had approved the stoning, what would have happened to him? If Jesus hadn't approved the stoning, what would he have been accused of?

- We don't know what Jesus was writing in the dust. Do you think it might have been the Ten Commandments?

- Who are the first ones to leave the scene?

- By not leaving with the crowd, what is Jesus saying about himself?

- Does Jesus condone the adultery? What do you think the thoughts of the woman were as she left?

- What do we learn about God from this?

- How can Christians reflect more of Jesus' attitude in the area of sex? ❑

Much of Paul's teaching on marriage comes in his first letter to the church in Corinth, a town where sexual immorality was widespread.

d) Read 1 Corinthians 6:9–20.

- From verses 9–11 what do you think was happening in the Corinthian church?

  - Is this similar to what we see happening in our own culture?

  - How does Paul view this sort of morality?

  - What challenge do these verses hold out to you?

  - What hope do they offer?

- From verses 12–20 it is plain that some members of the Corinthian church clearly felt that what they did with their bodies had no relevance to their faith.

  - Do people today believe that the spiritual and the physical worlds are separate?

  - What is Paul's response?

  - What reasons does he give in verses 19 and 20 for seeking sexual purity? ❑

6) PERSONAL STUDY

a) Read 1 Corinthians 7:1–8. This passage follows on from the previous one. In cultures that are obsessed by sex there is the danger of becoming as immoral as the surrounding world. But there is also the danger of rejecting sex in its rightful place.

- Is Paul positive or negative about sex?
- According to verses 3–5, which partner in a marriage has sexual rights?
- Do people think of sex in marriage as being unspiritual or impure? What would Paul say to this?
- In verse 10, what ruling does Paul make on divorce? ❏

b) Read Ephesians 5:21–33.

- What does it mean to submit to one another?
- What duty is imposed on the man in a marriage? Why is this hard? What should this mean in practice?
- What duty is imposed on the woman? Why is this hard?
- What causes of divorce and adultery would be eliminated if husbands and wives followed the pattern outlined here?
- Is this pattern an impossible ideal? Does Ephesians 5:18 'Don't be drunk with wine, because that will ruin your life. Instead, be filled with the Holy Spirit' offer any help? ❏

7) THE SUMMARY

a) Think about marriage:

- What according to the Bible is the purpose of marriage? How does that differ from the world's view of it?
- Why is marriage such a serious business?
- Christians have always been quick to condemn sexual sins; why have we been less effective about proclaiming the goodness of marriage?
- How can we affirm marriage without making singles feel isolated?
- How can we keep ourselves from being dragged down to the world's view of sex and marriage?
- If you are married, how can you help your marriage improve? ❏

b) Think about adultery:

- Why does the Bible view adultery as such a serious sin?
- It might be easy for many people to say that they have kept this commandment because they have not had sex with someone else's marriage partner. But if we look at it in the way that Jesus does, have any of us kept this?

- With theft we saw that restitution was possible. Can this be done with sexual sin?
- What practical steps can we take to avoid sexual sin? ❑

c) Discussion

i) What could you do in the following situations?

- You go into your local newsagent and see pornographic magazines on the middle shelves of the magazine rack. ❑

- You are watching the TV with your children and you realise that three out of the four adverts in an interval use highly sexual images and innuendo. ❑

- One of your married friends has become increasingly remote. You have a feeling that he has been developing an inappropriate relationship with a woman. You don't know that anything is happening but you are concerned. ❑

- At church there is a married man who is obviously flirty and far too familiar with women. He obviously makes people feel uncomfortable yet is in a position of responsibility. ❑

- A married friend comes to you to ask for your help. She says that she has found herself attracted to a man she is working with and she is aware that he is attracted to her. ❑

ii) What do you think the local church could do to help the following groups of people?

- Those who are married
- Those who are young and single
- Those who are older and seem set to spend the rest of their life as singles
- Those Christians who are struggling with a homosexual orientation ❑

d) So what?

At the end of this study:

- What has challenged you most?
- In what areas are you most vulnerable?
- What attitude or action do you need to change? ❑

8) STEPPING OUT

a) Practical suggestions

- Is there something in this area that you need to repent of?
- Is there someone that you need to apologise to?
- What specific actions do you need to take to help keep this commandment?
- If you suddenly found yourself facing a major sexual temptation, do you have someone who you feel you could talk to honestly? If not, why don't you ask God to grant you such a friendship? ❏

b) Further study

i) Leviticus 18:1–30 lays down the rules on sexual purity for God's people.

- The sort of large, close-knit families that existed in Old Testament times could easily have been the setting for wholesale sexual abuse. What lessons can we draw from these restrictions for our own culture?
- What things are condemned here that surprise you?
- These rules were given before the Israelites moved in to take the Promised Land from the Canaanites. According to verses 27–28 why are the Canaanites being expelled from the land? Can the Israelites repeat their sins? If they do what will happen? ❏

ii) Read Proverbs 5:15–20.

- What attitude to sex within marriage is taught here?
- What attitude to sex outside marriage is taught? ❏

iii) We have already looked at King David's disastrous adultery with Bathsheba. In 2 Samuel 13:1–22 we move forward a generation.

- Amnon says that he is in love with Tamar. Judging by what happens, is it really love?
- What does Tamar suffer?
- What does David do? What should he have done? Do you think his own past might have made him unable to discipline in this case?
- In fact, the repercussions of Tamar's rape are terrible; within a few chapters both Amnon and Absalom die violently and the

country is plunged into a bloody civil war. What does this tell us about lust?   ❏

Yet there is hope.

iv) Read Psalm 51.

- In view of the adultery and murder he has committed, do you think David has any right to come to God at all?
- Does he offer excuses?
- What does he ask God to do for him?
- Do we need to pray a prayer like this?   ❏

c) Questions to think about

i) Is it any of our business what those outside the church do with their sexuality?   ❏

ii) What seem to be the reasons for men committing adultery? What seem to be the reasons for women committing adultery?   ❏

9) FOR PRAYER

- The moral climate in the nation at the moment.
- The witness of Christians in this area.
- Christian marriages.
- Those in vulnerable and exposed positions.

STUDY 5
MANAGE YOUR ANGER

Commandment 6: *'You must not murder.'* (Exodus 20:13)

At first glance this appears to be a commandment that we do not need to study; we all know that murder is wrong and few of us are likely to commit it. Yet the scope of this commandment goes wider than murder and it has enormous implications for our society. And when Jesus deals with this commandment, he extends it so wide that none of us can escape its challenge.

PART ONE

1) STARTER

First,

a) Either:

Who has ever said any of the following?

'I'd kill him if I caught him.'

'People like that ought to be lynched.'

'I could have danced on her grave.'

'Drop dead!'   ❏

Or:

Who has been a victim or spectator of road rage, computer rage or something similar? What happened?

Then

b) Each member should recount briefly an occasion when they, or someone else, was really angry. Then they should say what the anger achieved.   ❏

2) SURGERY

Discuss at least one of the following:

a) Consider the following figures:

• Official statistics show that in 1950 there were 4,000 recorded offences of 'violence against the person' in England

and Wales. In 2006 – for a population only a fifth larger – there were 1,044,733.

- Almost half (44%) of all incidents reported by women in a survey on British crime were domestic violence incidents.
- It is estimated that over 500 million people lost their lives as a result of war and conflict during the last century. ❏

b) Does the threat of violence affect your lifestyle? Are there places you do not visit in order to avoid risk? ❏

c) Are there people whom you avoid dealing with because they get so angry? ❏

3) GROUP STUDY

This is divided into an Old and a New Testament part.

The Old Testament

The Old Testament teaching on murder is plain.

a) Read Genesis 1:26–27.
- How are human beings different from animals?
- What does it mean 'to be made in God's image'?
- Why then is killing human beings so serious? ❏

b) Read Genesis 4:1–12.
- How does Cain respond to God's rejection of his offering (v.5)?
- In verse 7 what imagery is used for sin? What does this passage seem to imply about the danger of anger?
- Who was Cain really angry with? So why did he murder Abel? ❏

After the Flood, God sets out a covenant with Noah that refers to murder.

c) Read Genesis 9:5–6.
- What does this tell us about God's attitude to murder?
- Capital punishment in the case of murder is commanded here. What is the reason given? ❏

Note: Christians differ over whether God's ruling here on capital punishment is to be enforced today.

---

d) Read Exodus 20:13.

Note: The Hebrew word that is translated in most modern versions as 'murder' means 'to unlawfully take a human life'. It is more restricted in scope than our word 'kill' but covers more than 'murder'.

- What in Israelite society would have been 'lawful killing'?
- In what ways do people unlawfully kill today?
- How might we express this commandment positively as 'You shall . . .'? ❑

4) PERSONAL STUDY

a) Read Deuteronomy 22:8. This law is one of a number of examples given in Deuteronomy that apparently set out legal principles that were followed in other cases.

- Who is held to blame for the accident? The person who fell off? God? The owner?
- Is this murder?
- What is the principle these verses proclaim?
- How ought this principle be applied in our lives? ❑

b) We saw the link between anger and murder in the story of Cain and Abel. Elsewhere in the Old Testament the book of Proverbs speaks about anger. Look in turn at Proverbs 14:29, 15:18, 19:11, 29:11.

In terms of anger:

- What characterises the fool?
- What characterises the wise person? ❑

c) The Bible also tells us that God gets angry! Read Exodus 32:2–10. The background to this is that the Israelites have only just been miraculously delivered from Egypt by the LORD.

- What have they done that makes God so angry?
- How does God's anger differ from Cain's anger in Genesis 4?

Two chapters later we get an insight into God's anger. Read Exodus 34:5–6.

- What do we learn about God's character here?
- What characteristics of God seem to balance his anger?

- Do we desire that verse 6b could be a description of us? ❑

The Old Testament points out that keeping this commandment is more than just avoiding acts of murder.

d) Read Leviticus 19:18.

- If we are not to seek revenge or to bear a grudge what must we do instead?
- What does the last sentence ('I am the LORD') imply with regard to this instruction? ❑

e) Read Proverbs 24:11–12

- What positive actions are we encouraged to take?
- What excuses are we to avoid?
- How might we apply this verse today? ❑

SUMMARY OF PART ONE

If, as recommended, you are spreading the study of this commandment over two weeks, try to end the first week here by summarising what you have learnt from the Old Testament passages you have studied. What issues have they raised?

PART TWO

REVISION OF PART ONE

If, as recommended, you are spreading the study of this commandment over two weeks, it is useful to try and spend a few minutes here reviewing what you learned the previous week in Part One before moving on to the New Testament.

5) GROUP STUDY

The New Testament

a) Jesus deals with this commandment in the Sermon on the Mount. Read Matthew 5:21–26.

- As we have seen, the Old Testament clearly condemned murder. How does Jesus go further?

- What does Jesus' restatement of this commandment say a) about harsh words? b) about angry thoughts?

- According to verses 23–25 which takes priority: worship or right relationships? Why? ❏

b) Read Matthew 5:38–48. The Law of Moses that Jesus refers to (Exodus 21:24, Leviticus 24:17–20) seems originally to have been intended – by limiting retribution – to stop any blood-feud escalating.

- What action does Jesus propose instead?

- In verse 43 Jesus repeats a popular saying; but does it quote the Old Testament accurately (see Leviticus 19:18)? How do you suppose the saying had arisen?

- In verse 44 is Jesus contradicting the Old Testament or extending it?

- How does God treat evil people (v.45)? What do we have to do to be his children?

- What does this passage suggest about anger, hatred and murder? ❏

> NOTE: Jesus appears here to be talking only about how we personally should act. There is no indication that he is laying down rules for how society should work. Indeed the assumption in the New Testament is that societies will always have law courts and punishment systems.

c) Read Matthew 6:14–15.

- What is the promise in these verses?
- What is the warning?
- Can we forgive and still be angry? ❏

d) Read Matthew 5:9–11.

- What would it mean to carry this out in a family feud or a business dispute?
- What might we expect to be the result for us personally (see Matthew 5:11)?

Jesus, however, also showed anger. ❏

e) Read Mark 3:1–6.

- What was the attitude of Jesus' enemies to a) Jesus, b) the man with the deformed hand, c) the law about the Sabbath?
- Why was Jesus angry? ❏

6) PERSONAL STUDY

a) Read John 2:13–16.

- What should have been going on in the temple?
- What was going on instead?
- What effect might this business activity have had on someone who had come to the temple to seek God?
- Under what sort of conditions might anger be acceptable for a follower of Jesus today? Give some examples. ❏

b) Paul also talks about anger and its dangers. Read Ephesians 4:25–32.

- In verse 26 what two rules on anger does Paul give?
- What, according to Paul, in verse 27, is the great danger in anger?
- In verses 31–32, what alternatives to anger does he suggest? ❏

c) Read James 1:19–20.

- What remedy for anger does James suggest in verse 19?
- Why, in verse 20, is anger condemned? How should that encourage us to stay calm? ❏

d) Read 1 John 3:15–17.

- Why is hatred between Christians an appalling thing?
- What is the standard to be for our relationships as Christians?
- What is the link between verse 17 and the previous two verses? ❏

e) Read Romans 13:9–10

- Does Paul suggest that this commandment be abolished?
- How is it – and the others – to be kept?
- What does that mean in practice? ❏

7) THE SUMMARY

a) Think about anger and murder:

- How does the world view the value of a human life? What, according to the Bible, is its value?
- What actions are we to avoid if we are to keep this commandment?
- Is avoiding unlawful killing in all its forms enough? What more, according to Jesus, must we do?
- How often does our anger achieve anything useful? How often does it do more harm than good? ❏

b) Think about love and forgiveness:

- Why is love and forgiveness the better way?
- Why is this way so hard?
- How can we encourage ourselves and others to show love and forgiveness? ❏

c) Discussion

i) What would you be tempted to do in the following situations? What ought you to do?

- Your boss angrily accuses you of failing to meet a deadline; you know it is because he failed to give you the time you needed. ❏
- A driver overtakes you wildly and cuts in dangerously just ahead of you. ❏

- A combination of road works causes you to be stuck in traffic a mile from work when you should be at an important meeting. ❏

- Despite repeated warnings your child's bedroom is a total mess. ❏

- A newspaper reveals, beyond a shadow of a doubt that government policy to a particular country is causing widespread starvation. ❏

ii) Popular wisdom still believes that anger can be good and that by being angry we are 'getting it off our chest' or 'clearing the air'. Can this be true? ❏

iii) A Christian friend is really angry over a serious injustice to them at their work. How might we advise them? ❏

iv) What would you think are the dangers of denying that you feel angry? ❏

d) So what?

At the end of this study:

- What has challenged you most?
- In what areas are you most vulnerable?
- What attitude or action do you need to change? ❏

8) STEPPING OUT

a) Practical suggestions

i) As you enter the week ahead try to be conscious of when you get angry. Let's call it an Anger Audit. Ask yourself these questions:

- What is causing me to get angry?
- Am I seeing the full picture?
- How might Jesus react in this situation?
- How can I express my anger without crushing others?
- What do I want to change as a result of this? ❏

ii) Locate one situation of conflict in the world and pray for peace there.

- Pray for an opportunity to be involved as a peacemaker in some conflict, either in the community, at home, or by supporting an issue in wider society.

- Pray for an opportunity to be a life giver. ❏

iii) Try to practise forgiveness.

- Examine your heart. Is there someone against whom you are harbouring anger? Seek forgiveness for yourself and ask for Christ's power to forgive them.

- Determine that you will try and forgive any wrongs that are done to you this week. In a week's time evaluate how you have done. ❏

b) Further study

i) Chapter 35 of the book of Numbers lays down the detailed rules for distinguishing between manslaughter (punishable by banishment) and murder (punishment by death). Read Numbers 35:30–34.

- There needed to be two witnesses to a crime for a murderer to be executed; what do you think this was to prevent?

- What does the fact that money could not pay for murder or manslaughter suggest about the value of life?

- What, according to verses 33 and 34 is the reason why murder must be so firmly dealt with? ❏

ii) Read 1 Chronicles 22:6–8. Although killing in warfare was allowed, what does this passage suggest about God's attitude to this? ❏

iii) Read John 1:14. What extra significance to human life does this passage add? ❏

c) Questions to think about

i) In the world of the Bible, killing was largely something that you carried out by hand-to-hand fighting. We have perfected methods of automated mass killing at a distance. What do you think Jesus or the prophets would say about our 'clean' wars? ❏

ii) Death in some shape or form is often proposed as a solution to problems. People abort unwanted babies, want the death penalty for murderers and consider mercy killing for the elderly.

- What should be the Christian response?
- Is it simply enough to oppose these things? ❑

iii) If all humans are made in the image of God then that includes us. How should the fact that we are made in the image of God affect how we feel about ourselves? ❑

9) FOR PRAYER

- The low value of human life in the nation and the world.
- Those doctors, nurses, judges and parents facing difficult issues of life and death.
- The high levels of anger in our society.

STUDY 6
KEEP PEACE WITH YOUR PARENTS

Commandment 5: *'Honor your father and mother. Then you will live a long, full life in the land the L*ORD *your God is giving you.'* (Exodus 20:12)

All societies are held together by links that run between people and between generations. This commandment concentrates on the most important of those links: the relationship between parents and children in the family.

The commandments we have looked at so far have dealt with issues of relationships between individuals. With this commandment we start to move inwards into the heart of our lives by looking at our relationship with our parents. As we move into this area we need to realise that, for many people, the topic of families is one filled with hurts, grief and guilt. Our families can be the source of some of our greatest blessings but they can also be the source of some of our deepest pains.

> LEADER'S NOTE: The atmosphere needs to be one of acceptance with no condemnation or judgementalism. It may well be that significant issues will come up in the course of the evening that will need ongoing prayer and ministry.

PART ONE

1) STARTER

a) Begin with giving one or two of these scenarios to members of the group to work through in pairs – then discuss them together. Be prepared for emotional issues to be raised.

- Your friend comes to tell you of their dilemma with their 16-year-old son. He asked them the other night if they would mind if he had his ear pierced. Your friends aren't keen on it. What would you advise? ❏

- A couple ask you for advice regarding a choice of possible career moves. The husband has been offered two possible jobs, one in the south of England and one in the north. The job in the south of England is in a nicer location with better schools, while the northern job is within thirty minutes' drive of her elderly parents. His parents have both died. They ask you what you think the responsible Christian decision would be. ❏

- A member of the youth group comes to ask you for your advice regarding her family situation. She explains that she comes from a family which is not churchgoing and which is increasingly hostile to her new-found faith. Her parents keep nagging her to stop going to youth group meetings, saying her work is suffering (which she denies), and are now saying they will refuse to sign the consent form for the youth group's summer camp. She wants to honour her parents. What should she do? ❏

- Some members of the church have decided to let their 17-year-old daughter, a pillar of the youth group, stay at home while they go away on a conference. They have agreed that she can have a couple of friends over to watch a DVD on the Saturday night. You find out accidentally that the teenagers are actually planning a large party. What do you do? ❏

- A friend is discussing the plight of his recently widowed father who has been left alone in a big, hard-to-maintain house over a hundred miles away. Your friend and his wife have a big house themselves, yet in the discussion there has been no mention of him coming to live with them. Do you suggest it? ❏

- One of your friends has two grown-up sons who have left home and a younger teenage daughter who is still living at home. The couple became Christians a couple of years ago and have since decided they brought their first two children up too liberally and need to be a lot stricter with their daughter. You are aware that their daughter is becoming increasingly resentful, rebellious and angry about this. What do you do? ❏

- A couple have two children. The husband's parents are extremely anxious that the children be sent to private school and are even offering to pay the fees. The couple do not want this and he is worried that to reject such an offer would fail to honour his father and mother. What do you advise? ❏

- A married couple in your church have come with a problem. They had made a decision not to try to have a family but have recently heard some people saying that such a decision is selfish. They ask you what you think. ❏

- At a church weekend away you notice a father regularly speaking harshly to his son. A couple of times you see him smack him in a manner that concerns you. You express your concern to someone else and are told that that father believes that he is helping the boy to honour him. Do you say anything to the father? If so, what? ❏

b) Have a number of volunteers say what they found hardest about honouring their parents. ❏

c) If there are any parents present ask them to share what they have found hardest about being parents. ❏

2) SURGERY

Discuss at least one of the following:

a) It has been claimed that the cost of family breakdown to the UK taxpayer was twenty billion pounds in 2006. How would these costs arise? Who is going to pay for them? ❏

b) Most social welfare (care, support, etc.) for people still occurs within families. Is it realistic that any state can afford to provide an alternative? ❏

c) You are writing a novel that features a vicious and scheming villain.

- What sort of family background would you invent for him (or her)?
- Is the common linkage of criminal behaviour to a bad family background stereotyping or does it have a basis in reality? ❏

3) GROUP STUDY

This is divided into an Old and a New Testament part.

The Old Testament

a) Read Exodus 20:12.

In the world of the Bible what would the social, economic and religious importance of the family have been? What responsibilities would parents have had towards their children?

- What would be your definition of 'honouring'? Is it the same as 'obeying' or 'respecting'?
- How could you dishonour your parents? Give examples.

- Why do you think this commandment mentions both father and mother?
- Israelite society was made up of families rather than individuals. Why in this case was the break-up of families so serious?
- This commandment has a blessing attached. Do you think that this is because God rewards people who honour their parents or is it because honouring parents leads to the sort of society where long happy lives occur? If families failed what would have been the implication for Israel's stay in the Promised Land? ❏

b) Read Leviticus 20:9.

- Is the crime here merely disobedience?
- What does this suggest about the importance of the family? ❏

Note: The Bible records no case of this penalty ever having been carried out.

c) Read Proverbs 13:24.

- What is the relationship between love and discipline?
- Should there be limits to discipline? What? ❏

d) Read Deuteronomy 6:4–7 and then Proverbs 22:6.

- What, according to these passages, is the vital duty of parents?
- Does this apply today? ❏

e) Read Leviticus 19:32.

- How does this broaden the commandment to honour parents?
- What is the link between reverence for God and respect for the elderly? ❏

4) PERSONAL STUDY

Read Ruth 1:1–18.

- What relation is Ruth to Naomi? What responsibilities does she take on?
- In what ways does Ruth act as a model for how children are to honour their parents? ❏

SUMMARY OF PART ONE

If, as recommended, you are spreading the study of this commandment over two weeks, try to end the first week here by summarising what you have learnt from the Old Testament passages you have studied. What issues have they raised?

PART TWO

REVISION OF PART ONE

If, as recommended, you are spreading the study of this commandment over two weeks, it is useful to try and spend a few minutes here reviewing what you learned the previous week in Part One before moving on to the New Testament.

5) GROUP STUDY

The New Testament

In his disputes with the Pharisees Jesus reinforced this commandment.

a) Read Matthew 15:1–9.

   The background to this passage seems to be that a practice had arisen by which money that should have been given to parents could be dedicated to God instead. It could then be recovered later, possibly after their deaths.

   • Although the Pharisees claimed the moral high ground over ritual washing, what does Jesus accuse them of?

   • Why does Jesus find their refusal to honour their parents particularly immoral?

   • What principle does Jesus lay down here about the relationship between religious duty and honouring our parents? ❑

   Jesus himself, however, knew only too well the problems that families can bring.

b) Read Mark 3:20–21,31–35.

   • Why does Jesus' family come to find him?

   • What are their concerns? Do you find them understandable?

   • Does Jesus obey them?

   • What principle does his response imply? ❑

   In his teaching Jesus warned his disciples of inevitable family tensions.

c) Read Matthew 10:32–39.

   • How might following Jesus cause a problem within a family?

   • Give some examples.

   • What family links does Jesus warn may be severed?

- What does this passage tell us about what our ultimate priority should be?
- Does Jesus imply that giving our loyalty to him will be painless or easy? ❏

d) Read John 19:23–27.

- List the different things that have happened to Jesus in the last few hours. What do his words in v.26 show about his priority now?
- Jesus' ministry appears to have been in spite of his mother's wishes (see Mark 3:20–21), yet now he arranges for her to be taken care of. What lessons can we draw from this for our relationships with our parents? ❏

e) Read Ephesians 6:1–4. This passage continues on from the passage on husbands and wives that we looked at in Study 4.

- What was the promise attached to this commandment in the Old Testament? How does Paul rework it? Why do you think he changes the wording?
- What is the duty that Paul places upon children?
- What is the duty that Paul places upon parents? ❏

NOTE: The wording in some Bible versions 'obey your parents in the Lord' has allowed some people to argue that this only applies to 'spiritual' parents and not to our human parents. In fact the NLT reading 'because you belong to the Lord' appears to better reflect the sense of the original.

6) PERSONAL STUDY

a) Read 1 Timothy 5:1–8.

- How does Paul say we are to treat the elderly?
- What should the church do with the vulnerable widow? What role is it to adopt?
- What does Paul say that neglect of needy relatives indicates?
- On the basis of this passage, is the church politically right wing (against handouts) or left wing (in favour of social care)?
- Does this sound like your church? Is this sort of welfare policy either needed or feasible in today's society? ❏

7) THE SUMMARY

a) Think about how we honour our parents:

- When, if ever, does this commandment expire?
- What are the limits to obedience?
- How do we honour an unworthy and unkind parent?   ❑

b) Think about how we are parents:

- Is this commandment only for children or does it also have a bearing on how parenting is to be done?
- How can parents treat their children in such a way as to make the keeping of this commandment easier?
- If a husband and wife are openly contemptuous to each other, can they expect respect from their children?   ❑

c) Think about the wider implications:

- What does this commandment say about the value of the family?
- If your own parents have died, are you now exempt from this commandment?
- Jesus passed on the responsibility for caring for his own mother to a disciple. Does this have implications for the care of those who cannot be taken care of by their own families?
- How can the church uphold the value of the family without seeming to be exclusive to those who are singles?
- The implication in the Bible seems to be that how we treat our parents is linked to how we treat God. Is this true?   ❑

d) Discussion

i) Some people are uneasy about the idea of God being their heavenly Father because of the problems they have had with their earthly father. How might we deal with this?   ❑

ii) What would you say to a teenager who came to you who was having a really hard time with their parents?   ❑

iii) What would you say to parents who came to you who were having a really hard time with their teenage children?   ❑

e) So what?

At the end of this study:

- What has challenged you most?

- In what areas are you most vulnerable?
- What attitude or action do you need to change? ❑

8) STEPPING OUT

a) Practical suggestions

i) Find some free time when you can be undisturbed and sit down and prayerfully evaluate your relationship with your parents.

- What is there to thank God for? Have you thanked God for it? Have you expressed your gratitude in any way to your parents? If you can, why not do it now?
- What is there in your relationship with your parents that needs either forgiveness or healing? What can you do to bring about any healing?
- Are there any duties to your parents (whether they are living or dead) that remain outstanding? ❑

ii) If you are a parent then, in a similar way, examine your relationships with your children.

- What is there to thank God for? Have you thanked God for it? Have you expressed your gratitude in any way to your children? If you can, why not do it now?
- What is there in your relationship with your children that needs either forgiveness or healing? What can you do to bring about any healing?
- Are you making time to talk with your children?
- Are there any duties or responsibilities to your children that remain outstanding? ❑

iii) In terms of your wider family, are there things that you can do to improve relationships? For example:

- When was the last family reunion you had?
- Is there some rift that you can help heal?
- Do you have isolated relatives who need visiting? ❑

iv) How can your church practically help in:

- Supporting parents in 'the most difficult job in the world' – that of bringing up children?
- Supporting young people in their responsibility to honour their parents?

- Taking a lead in being family to those without a family of their own? ❏

b) Further study

i) Read Proverbs 1:8,9.

- Whose moral teaching is a child to follow? What does this say about who does the teaching within a family?
- What is held out as being the reward of this parental teaching? ❏

ii) Read Luke 2:39–52.

- What does verse 41 teach us about the position of Jesus' parents towards their religious duties?
- From verses 49–51 what do we learn about Jesus' own attitude to a) God, and b) his parents?
- How is Jesus' position an example to us? ❏

c) Questions to think about

i) How does Jesus' relationship to his heavenly Father act as a model for us to honour our parents? ❏

ii) How is God's fatherly care of us a model for our own parenting? ❏

iii) Today, many people becoming believers in Jesus lack any personal experience of an effective, traditional family. Yet the church can often expect them to become perfect fathers or mothers overnight. Is this realistic? What alternative responses might we suggest? ❏

9) FOR PRAYER

- Pray for your own family. Pray that God would reveal to you what you can do to strengthen it.
- Pray for families that you know well. Pray specifically for good relationships within them.
- Pray that your church would be a source of support and encouragement to families.
- Pray that the national decline in the nature of family relationships would be reversed.

STUDY 7
STOP DRIVING YOURSELF CRAZY

Commandment 4: *'Remember to observe the Sabbath day by keeping it holy. You have six days each week for your ordinary work, but the seventh day is a Sabbath day of rest dedicated to the Lord your God. On that day no one in your household may do any work. This includes you, your sons and daughters, your male and female servants, your livestock, and any foreigners living among you. For in six days the Lord made the heavens, the earth, the sea, and everything in them; but on the seventh day he rested. That is why the Lord blessed the Sabbath day and set it apart as holy.'* (Exodus 20:8–11)

This commandment is all about our time. Time, like wealth, is a gift that God gives us and – like wealth – is something that he expects us to use wisely. And, as with wealth, God also expects that we honour him by returning to him at least a part of his gift.

There are aspects of this commandment that are unique. For the Christian a key aspect is that the fact that, unlike all the other commandments, this is not re-emphasised in the New Testament. Differing views have emerged on how Christians should treat this commandment. The three main positions are as follows:

- A small number of Christians (notably the Seventh Day Adventists) worship on Saturday in the belief that the church was mistaken in switching its holy day to Sunday.

- Another section of the church has felt that the Christian Sunday should retain much of the character of the Old Testament Sabbath. Believers in these churches mark Sunday by strictly abstaining from all work, recreation and sport.

- The position of the majority of Christians – and the view developed here – is that the Sabbath is part of the Old Testament Law that is now no longer binding on Christians. On this view the Sabbath regulations ('you must not do this or that') were fulfilled in Christ and have been abolished; however, the Sabbath principles (each week, we are to have a day where we especially honour God and take a break from work) still remain. In other words, while we are no longer required to keep the Sabbath, it is no bad thing that we allow ourselves a Sabbath.

PART ONE

1) STARTER

a) Either:

Have each member of the group quickly fill in the following list:

	Actual time spent (hrs a week)	Ideal amount (hrs a week)
Work (where employed)		
Travel		
Leisure		
Sport		
Shopping		
Housework		
Church meetings		
Relaxing		
Sleep		

(The total number of hours a week is 168)

- Does anybody have two columns that match?
- How do people feel about the discrepancy? ❑

Or:

Discuss briefly the following:

- Does your work control you or do you control your work?
- What is the longest you have ever worked without taking a day off?
- Do you feel guilty when you relax? ❑

b) Have different people give brief responses to each of the following dilemmas:

- You hear a Sunday newspaper will be publishing an article that greatly interests you. Do you buy the newspaper? ❑

- You have some special people coming for Sunday lunch and have put a lot of time and preparation into planning a meal. However, just before you go to church you realise you have forgotten an essential ingredient. You realise that you could buy it at the supermarket on the way back from church. What do you do? ❑

- A friend of yours has been out of work for some time and has at last been offered a job, but when he is sent the contract to sign he sees that it requires him to agree to work any Sunday that is demanded. What would you advise him to do? ❏

- Your church leader's wife has been offered a well-paid job that will require her to work every day except Sunday. As he is busy that day, they would have no shared day off. Should she take the job? ❏

- A relative comes to spend a Sunday with you. They go to church with you and as you come out of church they say, 'We've done what you wanted to do; now can I take you shopping? There are some things I really want to buy you.' Do you go together to the shops? ❏

2) SURGERY

Discuss one of the following:

a) Assuming that your group has people old enough to remember, have a few people briefly describe what a Sunday used to be like twenty, or even thirty years ago. ❏

b) What, if anything, have we lost with the decline of the traditional British Sunday? ❏

c) In what ways can work come to take the place of God? ❏

3) GROUP STUDY

This is divided into an Old and a New Testament part.

The Old Testament

a) Read Genesis 2:1–3.

- Why do you think God took a break from working?
- What does this teach us about a one-day-in-seven break?
- What do we learn from this about the nature of this seventh day? ❏

b) Read Exodus 16:11–30. Having been delivered from Egypt the Israelites are miraculously fed in the wilderness by manna.

- Why does manna need to be collected daily?

- What happens on the Sabbath? What happens on the day before?
- What does this passage teach is the purpose of the Sabbath?
- What are the people to do on it?
- What has God done to help them keep it? ❏

Note: These events took place before the Ten Commandments were given.

c) Read Exodus 20:8–11.

- What, according to this commandment, is the purpose of the Sabbath?
- What reason is given for the origin of the Sabbath?
- What are the people to do, and not to do, on the Sabbath?
- Why do you think foreigners and livestock are included in the commandment? ❏

Note: In the restatement of this commandment in Deuteronomy 5:15 the Israelites are told to remember on the Sabbath that the Lord their God had brought them out of Egypt. The Sabbath therefore came to commemorate both creation and redemption.

d) Later on in the book of Exodus the nature of the Sabbath is elaborated. Read Exodus 31:12–18.

- According to verses 13 and 17 what is the meaning of the Sabbath?
- Why do you think the breaking of the Sabbath is to be treated so seriously? ❏

e) Read Isaiah 58:13.

- What were the people to avoid doing on the Sabbath?
- According to this passage what sort of attitude were they to have towards the Sabbath?
- Do you see the Sabbath as it was given by God, as a blessing or as a burden? ❏

4) PERSONAL STUDY

Read Jeremiah 17:19–27.

- What was now taking place on the Sabbath?
- What does God promise will be the results if the Sabbath is respected?
- What does God warn will happen if the Sabbath is neglected? ❏

SUMMARY OF PART ONE

If, as recommended, you are spreading the study of this commandment over two weeks, try to end the first week here by summarising what you have learnt from the Old Testament passages you have studied. What issues have they raised?

PART TWO

REVISION OF PART ONE

If, as recommended, you are spreading the study of this commandment over two weeks, it is useful to try and spend a few minutes here reviewing what you learned the previous week in Part One before moving on to the New Testament.

5) GROUP STUDY

The New Testament

By the time of the New Testament the efforts to keep the Sabbath holy had produced 39 separate categories of banned actions with a long list of specifically banned acts in each category.

   a) Read Luke 4:14–16.

- What do we learn here about Jesus' normal practice on the Sabbath? ❏

   b) Read Mark 2:23 – 3:6.

- Why were Jesus' disciples breaking the Law? Did Jesus deny they were breaking the Law?

- What was the point that Jesus made about David?

- What did Jesus imply by saying that he was the Lord or Master of the Sabbath?

- Given the purpose for which the Sabbath was given, why do you think Jesus was angry about the rules that had come to surround this day?

- What principles does Jesus establish here about a) the Sabbath? b) his own relationship to it?

- What was the result of this confrontation? Why did it arouse so much hostility? If we are Jesus' disciples, what are the lessons for us? ❏

   c) Read John 5:2–18.

- In verse 17 what does Jesus admit that he is doing on the Sabbath?

- How does he justify himself? What does this say about who Jesus is? (Note the response in 5:18.)

- What do you think is the relevance of this for the way that Jesus' followers are to treat the Sabbath? ❏

There is evidence very early in the history of the church of worship on the Jewish Sabbath being gradually replaced by worship on the first day of the week (cf. Acts 20:7; 1 Corinthians 16:2).

d) Have different people read aloud John 20:1,19,26 and Acts 2:1–4.

- If the Old Testament Sabbath was a time to commemorate the creation of the world and the deliverance (or 'redemption') of Israel from Egypt, what extra things do you think that Christians would have remembered in their Sunday worship? ❏

When Gentiles started to become Christians, a major issue that surfaced was over which parts of the Old Testament Law the new converts should follow.

e) Read Colossians 2:16,17.

- What seems to have been the problem that Paul is addressing here?
- What does Paul say has replaced the Old Testament Law?
- What does this mean for celebrating Sabbaths? ❏

6) PERSONAL STUDY

a) In Galatia very zealous Jewish Christians began to teach the Gentile believers there that if they wanted to really follow Jesus they had to obey everything written in the Jewish Law. Paul's response to this situation is found in the letter to the Galatians. Read Galatians 4:3–12.

- In what way does Paul say that the Galatians had been slaves?
- How had they been freed?
- What were they doing by returning to their old practices?
- How should people who are free from the Law live?
- What does verse 10 suggest about how Christians are to view the Sabbath? ❏

The whole issue of what aspects of the Jewish Law were to be kept by Gentiles who became Christians soon faced the church leaders in Jerusalem. Acts 14 summarises the discussion among them and Acts 15 records the letter sent out as a result.

b) Read Acts 15:22–31.

- Although arguments from silence are notoriously suspect, what do you conclude from the absence of any mention of the Sabbath? ❏

Note: The reference to sexual immorality may be to the marriage of close relatives as prohibited in Leviticus 18.

c) Read Romans 14:5–13. There was clearly some variation in the Early Church over which day, if any, was kept holy.

- What, in verse 6, does Paul suggest should be the right attitude to these issues?
- What (in verses 10 onwards) does Paul suggest should be our attitude to those who take different views on these issues? ❏

d) Read Hebrews 10:24–25.

- Does our freedom from Sabbath rules mean that we have freedom to do anything we want?
- Why should we meet together? What is likely to happen if we do not? ❏

7) THE SUMMARY

a) Think about the principle of the Sabbath:

- For the Jew the signs of being in a covenant relationship with God were circumcision and keeping the Sabbath. What are they for the Christian?
- Breaking the Sabbath was all too easy for the Jewish believer; but how can Christians break the Sabbath?
- If we are no longer bound by the Law what principles should govern how we live on Sundays? ❏

b) Think about the nature of rest:

- How do you react to the idea that God is concerned that we take a rest?
- Are we cheating on a day of rest if, while resting we are continuously thinking about our work all the time?
- How can we balance keeping Sunday as a day of rest and having it as a day for worship?
- How can we recover the Old Testament idea that the Sabbath was to be a joyful day? ❏

---

c) Discussion

i) What would you say to someone who had just become a Christian and wanted to know what they should do on Sunday? ❏

ii) What might be different about the responsibilities and priorities for a day off for the following people:

- A 16-year-old college student.
- A single mother with two children.
- A father with a highly pressured job and 3 children.
- A retired couple who rarely see their grandchildren.
- The minister of a local church. ❏

iii) Think of the following situations:

- Angie watches sport on Sunday.
- Lara likes to go jogging on Sunday mornings before church.
- Bill kicks a ball around with his children on Sunday afternoons.
- Jim plays in the church football team, which often has an informal fun match against another church on a Sunday afternoon.
- Ted plays in an amateur league that plays on Sunday.
- Brian is a professional footballer and regularly plays Sunday matches.

Where, if anywhere, do you draw the line? ❏

iv) What do you say to someone with a busy week job who feels exhausted by all the church responsibilities that he or she faces on a Sunday? ❏

v) Imagine that in your church there is a firm conviction that the Sabbath laws do not apply to Sunday. You want to organise an inter-church sports event and Sunday afternoon seems the best time. However, one church you want to invite believes strongly that having such an event on Sunday would be sinful. Do you reschedule the event for another day? ❏

vi) You meet a Christian who is too busy playing sport to go to church more than once a month. He says he has been 'set free in Christ'. What would you say? ❏

d) So what?

At the end of this study:

- What has challenged you most?
- In what areas are you most vulnerable?
- What attitude or action do you need to change? ❑

8) STEPPING OUT

a) Practical suggestions

- Evaluate how you spend your day off. Are you using it rightly?
- What two things could you stop doing that would help you to use it better?
- What two things could you start doing that would help? ❑

b) Further study

i) Read Psalm 92:1–4. The title of this psalm makes it plain that this is a song for the Sabbath day.

- What is the mood of this psalm?
- What is its basic theme?
- What does this teach us about the way that a Sabbath ought to be observed? ❑

ii) Read Nehemiah 13:15–22. Here Nehemiah acts to remedy abuses of the Sabbath.

- What is taking place on the Sabbath?
- What does Nehemiah say was the result of profaning the Sabbath in the past?
- What practical action does Nehemiah take to preserve the Sabbath? ❑

iii) Read 1 Thessalonians 5:16–18.

- When are we to pray and praise God?
- What could this suggest about reserving all our worship for Sunday? ❑

iv) The Fourth Commandment also tells us that work is good and something that God expects us to do. Read Colossians 3:23.

- What, according to this passage, should characterise our
  attitude towards work? ❑

c) Questions to think about

i) Is your idea of what you do on Sunday something that you
have thought through or just something that you have inherited
or absorbed from others? ❑

ii) Is what happens on Sunday a matter only for Christians and
churches? Do we have any responsibility to society in general in
this matter? Should we try and persuade non-Christians to
keep Sunday special? How? ❑

iii) Does a collective day for everybody make sense any more?
Does it matter if some people take one day and others take
another? ❑

iv) What would be your ideal for Sunday? What practical steps
can you take to move towards it? ❑

v) For many of us Saturday is also a day off. Where does this fit
in? ❑

vi) We often think or say, 'It's my time, I'll do what I want with it.'
Is it our time? ❑

9) FOR PRAYER

- Pray for the way you use your time.
- Pray for the right attitude to work.
- Pray for the right attitude to leisure.
- Pray for others that they might be able to balance work, rest
  and worship.

STUDY 8
TAKE GOD SERIOUSLY

Commandment 3: *'You must not misuse the name of the LORD your God. The LORD will not let you go unpunished if you misuse his name.'* (Exodus 20:7)

If the Ten Commandments were a self-test quiz the Third Commandment is one that many of us might be inclined to tick off quickly. We don't blaspheme, we might say and, satisfied that this is one commandment that we do keep, we would move on.

Yet this is a commandment that, when looked at carefully, reveals vast and searching implications for the way that all of us use words.

PART ONE

1) STARTER

Either:

Share out one of the following scenarios to each of the group members. Each person is to outline the situation and suggest what their reaction would be:

- You are the headmaster of a historic school; two of your pupils have just been caught on the school grounds with drugs. ❑

- Your wife is a local councillor and at a dinner party you overhear someone say how greedy and corrupt all the councillors are. ❑

- A Christian you know made some reckless investments and has lost everything. Now he is claiming that 'the Lord led him to do it'. ❑

- You overhear someone claiming that he was the key person in setting up a very successful business deal. You know that, in reality, he got involved in the project only at a late stage. ❑

- You are the church treasurer and for weeks have been trying to persuade the minister that a new building project is unrealistic. One Sunday your church minister tells the congregation confidently that he believes it is God's will that the church go ahead with the programme. ❑

- You have just been interviewed by police over a major theft apparently committed by your brother. ❏

- You are the manager of an engineering firm and have just found out that one of your products has been made with substandard parts and will have to be the subject of a high profile public recall. ❏

- You are the minister of a church; the wife of a senior church figure has just made apparently genuine and very public allegations that he has physically abused her. ❏

- You are the captain of a naval destroyer docked in a Mediterranean port; two of your crew have been arrested after being involved in wrecking a local restaurant while drunk. ❏

Or:

Discuss the following:

a) Over breakfast you read in your paper that someone is producing a blasphemous film about Jesus. Do you:

- Decide to write to your MP?
- Decide to pray that it will fail at the box office?
- Decide to pray for God to judge the wicked?
- Shrug your shoulders and turn to the next page? ❏

b) You have had an awful week and you turn up at church feeling thoroughly down. The service starts off with a loud and cheerful song about how wonderful we feel because we know that Jesus loves us. Do you:

- Mouth the words?
- Force a smile and sing?
- Refuse to sing because you think it's the only honest response? ❏

2) SURGERY

Discuss one of the following:

a) How have you seen or heard the name of God or Jesus Christ being treated lightly these days? ❏

b) Why does God's name now seem to 'carry no weight'? What effects does this seem to have on society? ❏

c) Some people may know or have known churches where there was an awed and holy reverence for God that bordered on fear. Is this a good or bad thing? ❏

3) GROUP STUDY

This is divided into an Old and a New Testament part.

The Old Testament

In the world of the Bible your name was more than simply something that you were called; it expressed who you were and what you stood for.

a) A passage that helps us understand what the expression 'the Name of the LORD' means is to be found in Exodus chapter 3. Read Exodus 3:1–15. Here God reveals himself to Moses.

- In verse 6 who does God describe himself as? Why do you think he does this?

- In verse 14 God gives his name. 'I AM WHO I AM' or 'I AM THE ONE WHO ALWAYS IS' are the most probable translations.

  - What does this name suggest about how God relates to human beings? Does he need us?

  - What does this name suggest about how God relates to the future? Does he change?

- In verse 15 the name 'Yahweh' (translated as 'the LORD' in most English versions, or 'Jehovah' in some older translations) is given. This shortened form of 'I AM WHO I AM' is the personal name of God and the one that is behind the agreement or covenant with Israel that is at the heart of the Old Testament.

  - What is the difference between knowing someone important only by their title ('Sir', 'General' and so on) and being allowed to call them by their personal name?

  - How do you think Moses would feel about being given God's personal name?

  - How would knowing this help him in the task of leading God's people out of Egypt?

- From this whole passage, what impression do you think Moses was meant to have of the LORD/Yahweh?

- In an effort to ensure that they could not break this commandment Jews never pronounced the name of Yahweh and replaced it with the expression 'the LORD', a practice that has been passed into English. Do you think this is a solution to the challenge of this commandment? ❏

The psalms are full of encouragements to praise the name of the LORD.

b) Have four people read out the following:

  i) Psalm 8:1,9

  ii) Psalm 22:22

  iii) Psalm 96:1,2

  iv) Psalm 99:1–3

- In what way do these psalms suggest the name of God ought to be treated?

- Do we treat God's name in this way? ❏

4) PERSONAL STUDY

a) Read 1 Samuel 17:32–47. The background is that the armies of Israel under King Saul are being challenged by Goliath, the Philistine giant.

- From the language used (vv.36,43b,45, etc.) is this a purely political battle between two armies? What is at stake?

- What do you think David meant when he said that he attacked 'in the name' of the LORD of Heaven's Armies? Is this language we could ever use of our (hopefully less violent) Christian activities? ❏

b) Read Ezekiel 36:16–24.

- What allegation concerns God in verses 20 and 21?

- In the covenant the LORD had declared himself to be Israel's king. If the Israelites had stayed in exile what would that have said about him?

- What action does God say he will take to defend his own name? ❏

Abuses of God's name occur throughout the Old Testament

---

c) Read Leviticus 24:10–16,23.

- Why was blasphemy treated so seriously?
- Why do you think the whole community was to be involved in the punishment? ❏

d) Read Leviticus 19:12.

- What kind of thing do you think is being condemned here?
- Why is it a serious offence?
- What might a modern equivalent to this be? ❏

e) Read Isaiah 48:1,2.

- What is God's criticism here?
- Why is this offensive to him?
- Are similar sins possible today? ❏

f) Read Judges 11:29–39.

- How does Jephthah misuse the name of the LORD?
- What lessons are there for us here? ❏

SUMMARY OF PART ONE

If, as recommended, you are spreading the study of this commandment over two weeks, try to end the first week here by summarising what you have learnt from the Old Testament passages you have studied. What issues have they raised?

PART TWO

REVISION OF PART ONE

If, as recommended, you are spreading the study of this commandment over two weeks, it is useful to try and spend a few minutes here reviewing what you learned the previous week in Part One before moving on to the New Testament.

5) GROUP STUDY

The New Testament

Jesus treats this commandment about misusing God's name in his usual radical way.

a) Read Matthew 5:33–37.

- What do you think was the problem with making vows in the name of the LORD? (Remember the story of Jephthah?)

- Clearly vows that used an alternative to the LORD's name were felt to be easier to break. What, however, does Jesus say about making any vow?

- What sort of lives must we live if we can't back up our promises with a solemn oath?   ❏

Note: The general consensus here is that Jesus is not forbidding formal oaths such as those taken in a court of law but those made to boost promises or threats.

b) Read Matthew 6:9.

- What does it mean to honour or hallow God's name?

- How is this the opposite of misusing God's name?

- Why are we to pray for this?   ❏

c) Read Matthew 7:21–23.

- How do the people described here misuse God's name?

- What is the judgement that they will suffer?

- Is this a danger for us? How can we avoid it?   ❏

d) Read Philippians 2:9–11.

- What does it mean that the name of Jesus is above every other name?

- How will the value of the name of Jesus be illustrated in the future?

- Do we treat the name of Jesus as being sacred now?   ❏

6) PERSONAL STUDY

a) The Bible teaches that the name of Jesus has power but that this power must not be abused. Read Acts 19:13–17.

- In what way were these exorcists misusing Jesus' name?
- How, in less obviously supernatural areas than exorcisms, might people fall into a similar trap today?
- What was the result of this incident in terms of respect for Jesus' name? ❏

b) Paul gives another illustration of a misuse in Romans 2:21–24.

- What are these people claiming to be?
- What are they in reality? What is the result?
- Give an example of how this might happen in a church situation today. ❏

7) THE SUMMARY

a) Think about how we can dishonour God's name:

- Do we ever use the name of God or Jesus without thinking about what we are saying?
- When we say 'Amen' to a prayer, do we realise that we are effectively committing ourselves to what it says?
- Are we ever frivolous or careless about our worship?
- If we are known to be Christians it means that we publicly bear Christ's name. Are we careful how we live in case a public sin or failing drags him down with us?
- Does the way that our church handles itself bring honour or shame to the name of Jesus? ❏

b) Think about how we can honour God's name:

- Do we ever give something or someone else the credit when it really belongs to God?
- Do our churches (doubtless inadvertently) ever promote themselves more than Jesus?
- Do we encourage people to engage in acts of worship (prayer, praise, taking communion) without them thinking about what they are saying, singing or doing? ❏

c) Discussion

i) There are one or two examples in the Bible of curses (e.g. 1 Corinthians 16:22). Would it ever be right to curse someone? ❏

ii) If we are in a difficult situation (perhaps, say, asked to contribute in a complex debate) is it best to stay silent rather than run the risk of dishonouring God by saying something stupid? ❏

iii) How do we balance a 'fear of the Lord' with an awareness of God's love towards us? ❏

d) So what?

At the end of this study:

- What has challenged you most?
- In what areas are you most vulnerable?
- What attitude or action do you need to change? ❏

8) STEPPING OUT

a) Practical suggestions

- Is your life consistent with your label? Is there a gap between your beliefs and your behaviour? Seek to bridge that gap. ❏

- Watch your language! Are the words that you use acceptable to God? Is the way that you say things acceptable to God? ❏

- Are you known as a person of your word? ❏

- Pay attention to how you sing or pray. We all have slips of concentration but do our hearts really mean what our lips say? ❏

- Do you give God all the glory when good things happen or do we try and grab a bit of it for ourselves? ❏

- Are you giving God adequate credit for all he has done and is doing for us? ❏

- Are you blaming God for something that is not his fault? ❏

b) Further study

i) Read Exodus 34:5–7. In this passage the Lᴏʀᴅ defines who he is and what his name means.

- What is there here to encourage us to approach God?
- What is there here to challenge us to respect God? ❏

Note: Verse 7b reflects the fact that, unless we let God deal with it, sin has repercussions that go beyond our own generation. This comes up in the next study.

ii) Read Isaiah 9:6. The prophet Isaiah here looks forward to the coming Messiah and predicts what he will be called.

- What is the difference between a name and a title?
- How does Jesus live up to these titles? ❏

iii) Read Matthew 1:20–23.

- What two names are given to the child here?
- How are they prophetic of Jesus' coming ministry? ❏

Note: Jesus is the Greek form of Joshua or Yeshua, which means Yahweh saves.

iv) Read Acts 4:11–12.

- What does this tell us about the proper use of the name of Jesus? ❏

c) Questions to think about

i) When we pray for something in Jesus' name but don't really believe that God will answer our prayers, aren't we misusing the name of Jesus? ❏

ii) Someone who is not a Christian tells you that they intend getting married in a Christian ceremony even though they do not believe in God. Is this an innocent mistake or a dangerous misuse of God's name? ❏

iii) Do we dishonour God when we take communion without thinking? (See 1 Corinthians 11:29.) ❏

9) FOR PRAYER

- Pray that we honour God and all that he stands for.
- Pray that our lives would bring God honour and not shame.
- Pray that there would be a respect and reverence for God's name and God's word in our land.

STUDY 9
KNOW THE REAL GOD

Commandment 2: *'You must not make for yourself an idol of any kind or an image of anything in the heavens or on the earth or in the sea. You must not bow down to them or worship them, for I, the LORD your God, am a jealous God who will not tolerate your affection for any other gods. I lay the sins of the parents upon their children; the entire family is affected – even children in the third and fourth generations of those who reject me. But I lavish unfailing love for a thousand generations on those who love me and obey my commands.'* (Exodus 20:4–6)

The first two commandments cover how we worship God; the first commandment deals with who we worship as God and the second commandment deals with how we worship God. In fact, this second commandment is more concerned with how we are not to worship God.

In our twenty-first-century Western world we are inclined to think of idolatry as a Stone Age crime; something that we have evolved beyond. Yet, as has been widely pointed out, *Homo sapiens* is a worshipping species and our hearts, minds and lives all too readily find something else other than the one true and living God to bow down before. That idolatry is a real risk is apparent from the Bible; there are more references to this commandment in its pages than to any other.

PART ONE

1) STARTER

Discuss either of the following:

a) Have each group member take one of the following substitutes and briefly outline their advantages over the real thing.

- Plastic flowers
- A good computer simulation of a car racing competition
- A robotic dog
- Fake pearls
- Online virtual friends
- Playing a CD of a concert
- An exercise bike
- Watching a TV soap (rather than getting involved in the real world)

- A software program that makes your computer look like a fish tank
- Online shopping
- Watching the big match on TV ❏

b) A hundred years ago what was the most splendid building in your town or city? What is the largest recent building in your town today? Do you feel that this says anything about your town? ❏

2) SURGERY

Discuss one of the following:

a) If you were allowed to make up your own religion, what rewards, promises and requirements would it include? How would you have God behave towards you? ❏

b) Many people are seriously discontented with their lives? What are the causes of this discontent? ❏

3) GROUP STUDY

This is divided into an Old and a New Testament part.

The Old Testament

a) Read Exodus 20:4–6.

- From verses 4 and 5 what seems to be the definition of an idol?

- Why would someone bow down before something they had made? What sort of justification might they make for this practice?

- God describes himself as jealous for our affection.

  - In what sort of human situation today might we hear of people 'being jealous for someone's affection'? Is that comparable to God's relationship to us?

  - Why do you think God is jealous? For his good? Or for our good?

- What, according to verse 5, appears to be the alternative to worshipping (or loving) God? Can't we be allowed to be somewhere halfway between the two?

- Do you see God 'punishing the children' as a statement of vindictiveness or as a statement that sin has a domino effect; its results echo on for generations?

- Do you think that this is an irreversible curse? *
- How long is a thousand generations? What does a comparison of verses 5 and 6 suggest about God's character? ❏

b) Read Exodus 32:4–9. Note that the Israelites had only just left Egypt where the gods were often represented by animals.

- Moses had been gone for weeks up the mountain. What do you think was the mood amongst the people?
- As Moses' deputy, how do you imagine Aaron felt? Why do you suppose he made an image? How do you think he would have justified what he did?
- Do you think the ensuing worship was pagan, Jewish or mixed?
- What is God's verdict on the episode? ❏

c) There are many passages in the Old Testament Prophets that talk about the sin of idolatry. Read Jeremiah 10:1–16.

- What are the idols unable to do (v.4–6)?
- What, in comparison, can the LORD do?
- Why, when they are so feeble, do you think people worshipped idols? ❏

4) PERSONAL STUDY

Idolatry can, however, be subtle, as two examples in the Old Testament make clear.

a) Read Numbers 21:4–9 and 2 Kings 18:1–4.

- How had the bronze snake been a blessing in the past?
- How should it have been treated? What happened instead? Why?
- What does Hezekiah do to it?

*Some people are concerned that they could be punished for sins committed by parents or grandparents. In fact in Jeremiah 31:27–34 God specifically says that under the new covenant this principle will not apply (verses 29–30). He also states that there will be forgiveness of sins (verse 34). Those under this covenant, which was brought in by Jesus (see 1 Corinthians 11:25), need therefore have no fears in this area. Nevertheless, the effects of sin do cross generations; ask any child of an alcoholic.

- Can you think of a situation where an object or institution that brought blessing in one generation became dangerously idolised later? ❏

b) Read 1 Samuel 4:1–11. The Ark was the chest where the Ten Commandments and other symbols of the covenant were kept. Much earlier, in the battles for the conquest of the Promised Land, it had often accompanied the armies.

- What was the Ark supposed to signify to the Israelites?
- How was the Ark viewed here (v.3)?
- How has the Ark become an idol?
- What lessons are there for us here? ❏

SUMMARY OF PART ONE

If, as recommended, you are spreading the study of this commandment over two weeks, try to end the first week here by summarising what you have learnt from the Old Testament passages you have studied. What issues have they raised?

PART TWO

REVISION OF PART ONE

If, as recommended, you are spreading the study of this commandment over two weeks, it is useful to try and spend a few minutes here reviewing what you learned the previous week in Part One before moving on to the New Testament.

5) GROUP STUDY

The New Testament

On the surface there is little relevant to the issue of idolatry in Jesus' ministry and teaching. After being exiled because of their idolatry the Jews had learned their lesson and were strictly opposed to any form of image that could be idolatrous. But idolatry can occur without images . . .

a) Read Matthew 6:24.

- What does Jesus say here is impossible?
- Why is it impossible?
- Why does money make such a potent idol?   ❑

b) As we saw earlier the most dangerous idols can come from 'holy things'. In discussion with a Samaritan woman about the right place of worship, Jesus makes a crucial prophecy. Read John 4:19–24.

Note: Jews and Samaritans differed over where the acceptable site to worship God was.

- What, says Jesus in v.21, is going to happen to affect the status of these places of worship?
- Jesus points out that it is the right manner of worship, not being in the right place, that is the most important thing. What definition of 'right worship' does he give?
- What does this suggest about how we worship?   ❑

c) The issue of idolatry surfaces later in John's gospel just after Lazarus is raised from the dead. Read John 11:45–53.

- What, according to verse 48, is the fear of the Pharisees?
- What should have been their response to what Jesus has done?
- What do they end up putting before their own Messiah?
- How could it happen that ensuring the survival of a religious system came before Christ?

- Did this form of idolatry die out in the first century or is it still a danger? ❏

6) PERSONAL STUDY

a) Once the church had spread into the Roman and Greek world it came face to face with widespread idolatry. Read Acts 17:16–31. Paul is on an unplanned trip to Athens.

- What is Paul's attitude to the idols around the city (v.16)?
- Why does he say that idolatry is wrong (vv.24,29)?
- Why, according to Paul, is the age of tolerating idols now over? ❏

b) Read Colossians 3:5.

- What, according to this verse, is idolatry?
- How are we to deal with it? ❏

c) Read 1 John 5:21 (NIV or NLT footnote).

- Why do you think the Apostle John considers idolatry so serious that he ends his letter with a warning against it? ❏

7) THE SUMMARY

a) Think about how we can make idols:

- Do we put things other than God first in our lives?
- Do we have an inadequate idea of who God is?
  Do we limit him?
- Do we try to make God into the sort of God that we want him to be?
- Are there rituals in the way we worship that we feel are especially 'holy'? ❏

b) Think about how we can worship the real God:

- Are we able to recognise God's gifts, and to praise the Giver not the gift?
- Are we content with letting God do what he wants to do? Or have we limited him?
- Do we let Scripture control our view of who God is? ❏

c) Discussion

i) Why does God not like us to try and make an image of him? If we could make an idol the size of the universe would it be more acceptable? ❏

ii) God is concerned that we have a 'right-sized' God. Is that for our benefit or his? ❏

iii) Some Christian counselling methods suggest that, in difficult circumstances, we try and imagine Jesus sitting or standing next to us. Is this idolatry? ❏

iv) How do we distinguish between having appropriate reverence for, say, the Bible or Communion without making idols out of them? ❏

d) So what?

At the end of this study:

- What has challenged you most?
- In what areas are you most vulnerable?
- What attitude or action do you need to change? ❏

8) STEPPING OUT

a) Practical suggestions

- Praise is one way of reminding ourselves who God really is and the best antidote to idolatry. This is probably why so many of the passages of the prophets that attack idols do so in the context of praise for God's greatness (i.e. the Jeremiah 10 passage looked at earlier). Take time out with the Psalms. ❏

- Do a spiritual audit. When you have spare moments, what does your mind drift to? What do you spend your money on? These questions probably point to where your heart lies. You may need to work at destroying your idols! ❏

- Ask yourself this: Who do I serve? Who controls me? If the answer is not God then you ought to look hard and prayerfully at how you live. ❏

b) Further study

i) Read Deuteromony 4:15–31.

- According to verses 15 and 16 why is trying to make an image of God a mistake?

- What, according to verse 23, will be the serious consequences of making idols?
- In verse 29 what hope is held out to idol worshippers? ❏

ii) Read Isaiah 44:6–20 (preferably in a modern version such as the NLT which captures the sarcasm).

- What do we learn about who the LORD is in verses 6–8?
- What, in contrast, are idols? Why is worshipping them futile? ❏

iii) In a brief passage in 1 Corinthians Paul touches on idol worship. Read 1 Corinthians 10:19–26.

- What does Paul say that these idols are not?
- What does he say that they are?
- What practical implications does he draw for the Corinthians in their pagan culture? ❏

iv) Read 1 Timothy 6:15–16 and John 14:8–11.

- What reasons does Paul give to Timothy as to why we cannot make an image of God?
- How does Jesus fulfil the need for us to have any such image? ❏

c) Questions to think about

i) Should church windows have stained-glass images? ❏

ii) Should actors play Jesus in films? ❏

iii) Imagine someone becomes a Christian in a household where there are real idols; what should he or she do? ❏

iv) The goals set by a government tend to be those of employment and economic growth rather than righteousness. Are these idolatrous? ❏

v) You are a church leader in another country. A number of short-tempered and muscular men with dark glasses draw your attention to the fact that the picture of the President is not to be found in the church. What do you do? ❏

9) FOR PRAYER

- Pray that we may honour God, and only God.
- Pray that we would be able to discern what the idols in our lives are and how best to deal with them.
- Pray that the leaders of our land would seek God's kingdom and his righteousness for our nation.

STUDY 10
LIVE BY PRIORITIES

Commandment 1: *'You must not have any other god but me.'* (Exodus 20:3)

The Second Commandment dealt with worshipping God in the right way. The First Commandment, however, comes to the heart of things; it is about making sure that we worship the right God and no one else. God wants a relationship with us but he is only prepared to be involved in one that is totally exclusive.

PART ONE

1) STARTER

Discuss some of the following:

- Imagine that your house catches fire. After ensuring that your family and pets are safe, what do you rush in to save? ❏

- You decide to look for a new job. What things would you consider to be either essential or desirable (salary, new car, responsibility, etc.)? ❏

- Who are the most committed members of any religion you have ever met? Why? ❏

- Who have you known, or heard of, whose desires ended up destroying them? ❏

2) SURGERY

Discuss one of the following:

a) Let's define religion as 'that which gives a life meaning or purpose'. On this basis:

- What are the main religions in your area?
- What demands of time or money do they make on their devotees?
- Where and what are their temples?
- What rites or practices do they carry out? ❏

b) Everybody likes to think that they are free and able to choose to do whatever they want. Is this an illusion? Doesn't everybody serve something or someone? ❏

---

3) GROUP STUDY

This is divided into an Old and a New Testament part.

The Old Testament

a) Read Exodus 20:1–3. Although verse 3 is normally considered the first of the commandments, the verses immediately before it are helpful in understanding what this commandment really means. As we saw in Study 8, behind the expression 'the LORD' lies the name 'Yahweh', the personal name of the God who had made a covenant with the Israelites.

- The covenant was God's solemn agreement to protect and bless the Israelites. Why do you think God starts the commandments by using his covenant name and reminding the people that he has just saved them out of Egypt?

- Do you think the commandments were a) rules someone had to keep in order that God would love them? b) the appropriate response to being one of God's saved and loved people? Which category do they fit into for Christians?

- Someone might say, 'Why can't God share worship with other gods?' How would you answer?   ❏

b) In Joshua 24 we read how, once established in the Promised Land, Joshua led the Israelites in a ceremony where they renewed their covenant vows. Read Joshua 24:1–28.

- What, according to verses 2–13, has the LORD done for the Israelites?

- What does he expect as a response?

- In verse 19 Joshua appears to express reservations about the people's reply. Is he a pessimist or a realist?

- How does this whole passage underline the seriousness of the commitment that the LORD expects of his people?

- How often does the word 'serve' or 'served' occur in this passage? Does this just mean they had an obligation to worship him? What would it have meant for the Israelites to serve God? What does it mean for us?

- What – if any – ceremonies of covenant renewal do Christians hold?   ❏

c) But who is this God that we are called to serve exclusively? Isaiah gives something of an answer. Read Isaiah 40:18–31.

- What does this passage say about the temptation we have to worship either things that we have made (vv.18–20) or things that we have done (vv.23,24)?
- How is God superior to either our idols or our achievements?
- What practical application of these truths is found in verses 27–31? ❑

4) PERSONAL STUDY

The exclusive bond that God wants with his people not only rules out the worship of other gods, it also rules out religious practices that would undercut that right relationship. Read Deuteronomy 18:9–14.

- What things are forbidden here?
- Why, in the light of the First Commandment, do you think they are prohibited? ❑

SUMMARY OF PART ONE

If, as recommended, you are spreading the study of this commandment over two weeks, try to end the first week here by summarising what you have learnt from the Old Testament passages you have studied. What issues have they raised?

PART TWO

REVISION OF PART ONE

If, as recommended, you are spreading the study of this commandment over two weeks, it is useful to try and spend a few minutes here reviewing what you learned the previous week in Part One before moving on to the New Testament.

5) GROUP STUDY

The New Testament

Much of what Jesus taught focused on the need to make God the centre of our lives; in order to become part of the kingdom of God we have to allow God to be king.

a) Jesus himself was specifically tempted over this commandment. Read Matthew 4:8–10.

   • Given the size of the offer that the Devil makes, how important do you think it was to him to break Jesus' commitment to the First Commandment?

   • Why does Jesus quote Scripture (Deuteronomy 6:13) back to the Devil?

   • What lessons are there here for us in regard to our commitment to worship and serve God? ❏

b) Read Matthew 22:34–40. Jesus is here quoting the verses from Deuteronomy 6:4,5 that lay at the heart of the Jewish faith.

   • What does verse 37 say is our duty towards God?

   • If we take this seriously where, when and how are we to love God?

   • What would that mean practically for us?

   • Can we keep this standard? ❏

c) The key issue is how we can get into that right relationship with God where he is central in our lives. Read what Jesus says to his disciples in John 14:20–24.

   • What is the relationship between Jesus and God (v.20)?

   • What is the relationship between Jesus and his disciples (vv.20,21)?

   • What is the test of whether we really love Jesus (vv.21,23a)?

   • How does the promise of verse 23b fulfil the requirement of the First Commandment? ❏

6) PERSONAL STUDY

Read 1 John 2:1–6.

- If we fail to keep the commandments, is there any hope for us?
- What has Jesus done to help us?
- Are we then free from the commandments?
- How then are we to live (v.6)? ❏

7) THE SUMMARY

a) Think about how we are only partially committed to God:

- What things compete with God in our lives? Do we see them as being other gods?

- What parts of our lives are there that God has no control over?

- Is our half-heartedness because we lack faith that God cares for us?

- Is our half-heartedness because we don't think that God is that important? ❏

b) Think about how we can be more fully committed to God:

- Are we really prepared to let God have that exclusive relationship that he wants?

- How can we be single-minded about serving God?

- How can we help each other to serve God more faithfully? ❏

c) Discussion

i) We like to think of ourselves as being free people, able to choose what we want to do. But is anybody free? The Bible portrays us as slaves to desires that we cannot control and which ultimately destroy us. Is serving God the only way to freedom? ❏

ii) The Bible is anxious that we realise that God is majestic and all-powerful. What price do we pay for having a small-sized God? ❏

iii) Some of our songs and our worship can make it seem as if loving God is something that only involves the emotions. Is this right? ❏

iv) We often relegate God to a compartment of our lives, marked 'Religion', which can stay shut for much of the time. How can we let 'God be God' in our lives? ❏

d) So what?

At the end of this study:

- What has challenged you most?
- In what areas are you most vulnerable?
- What attitude or action do you need to change? ❏

8) STEPPING OUT

a) Practical suggestions

- Review your relationship with God. How well do you know him? Are there things that need to be sorted out? ❏

- Think about some recent decisions you have made and actions you have taken. Did your relationship with God play any part in them? Think about decisions ahead; how can you ensure that God is allowed to play a part? ❏

- If your spiritual health was given a check-up, what would the verdict be? That you should give up unhealthy habits? Take more spiritual exercise? Take remedial medicine? Have radical surgery? ❏

b) Further study

i) Read 1 Kings 18:16–40. At this time the religion of Baal had almost taken over the worship of the one true God in Israel.

- Baal was a thunder god and Carmel was a site for the worship of Baal. Why do you think that Elijah chose to challenge his opposition this way? Are there lessons for us in dealing with 'other gods'?
- What was the challenge that Elijah threw down to the people in verse 21? Are they unable to choose? Or are they reluctant to make an exclusive commitment to the LORD?
- Elijah commanded that the prophets of Baal be executed. There could be no legitimate basis for such an act today, but what principles can we draw from this about how we should treat those things in our life that come between us and God? ❏

ii) Read Luke 8:15. Jesus explains what happens to the seed that fell on fertile ground in the Parable of the Sower.

- What does Jesus say is the secret of the fruitful life?
- How does this relate to the First Commandment? ❑

iii) Read Luke 12:13–21.

- What, according to this parable, is our ultimate priority?
- Why is anything else foolishness? ❑

iv) Romans 1 is the classic passage on how human beings fail to keep the First Commandment and what happens as a result. Read Romans 1:18–32. According to verses 18–25 God has given all humanity some knowledge of himself.

- How has this knowledge been treated?
- What, according to verses 26–32, has resulted from this? ❑

c) Questions to think about

i) If God spoke directly to us from heaven we would probably obey him instantly. But we generally treat his communication to us through the Bible as something less serious. Why? ❑

ii) Why is it so tempting to worship God and my career, God and my home or God and my wealth? Why does God have to demand an exclusive relationship? ❑

iii) Do people become like whatever god they worship? ❑

iv) It is easy to make grand declarations along the lines of 'I love Jesus so much that I would die for him.' Yet in practice it is often the little things that seem so difficult: making time to pray, being a law-abiding driver, not answering back to abuse and so on. How can we convert the principle into day-to-day practice? ❑

9) FOR PRAYER

- Pray that we would put God first in our lives.
- Pray that we would love God with our hearts, minds and actions.
- Pray that churches across the land would wake up to the responsibility to be totally committed to God.